D1080450

# THE
# MANCHESTER
# UNITED
## STORY

**A Pillar Box Red Publication**

©2016. Published by Pillar Box Red Publishing Limited, under licence from Bauer Consumer Media Limited. Printed in China.

This publication has no connection with the club, or clubs, featured, or with any organisation or individual connected in any way whatsoever with the club, or clubs, featured.

Any quotes within this publication which are attributed to anyone connected to the club, or clubs, featured have been sourced from other publications, or from the internet, and, as such, are a matter of public record.

Whilst every effort has been made to ensure the accuracy of information within this publication, the publisher shall have no liability to any person or entity with respect to any inaccuracy, misleading information, loss or damage caused directly or indirectly by the information contained within this book.

The views expressed are solely those of the author and do not reflect the opinions of Pillar Box Red Publishing Limited or Bauer Consumer Media Limited. All rights reserved.

ISBN: 978-1-907823-71-8

Images © Action Images.

**HISTORY OF FOOTBALL**

# THE MANCHESTER UNITED STORY

### IAIN SPRAGG

Edited by James Bandy of MATCH

# CONTENTS

| | | | |
|---|---|---|---|
| 6 | Introduction | 38 | 1955-56 Division One trophy |
| 10 | 1880s | 40 | 1956-57 Division One trophy |
| 11 | 1890s | 42 | Tommy Taylor |
| 12 | 1900s | 46 | 1960s |
| 14 | 1907-1908 Season | 48 | 1963 FA Cup |
| 16 | Billy Meredith | 50 | Denis Law |
| 20 | 1910s | 51 | 1964-65 Division One trophy |
| 21 | 1920s | 52 | George Best |
| 22 | 1930s | 54 | 1966-67 Division One trophy |
| 23 | Scott Duncan | 56 | 1968 European Cup |
| 24 | 1940s | 58 | Top Ten Home Wins |
| 25 | Sir Matt Busby | 62 | 1970s |
| 26 | 1948 FA Cup final | 64 | Manager profiles: Wilf McGuinness, Sir Matt Busby and Frank O'Farrell |
| 30 | 1950s | 66 | Tommy Docherty |
| 32 | 1951-52 Season | 67 | 1973-74 |
| 34 | Duncan Edwards | 68 | 1974-75 |
| 36 | All-Time Top Appearances | 70 | 1977 FA Cup final v Liverpool |

| | | | |
|---|---|---|---|
| | | 116 | 1999-2000 |
| 72 | 1977 FA Cup | 117 | Dwight Yorke |
| 73 | 1977 Charity Shield v Liverpool | 118 | 2000-2001 League |
| 76 | 1980s | 120 | 2002-03 Premier League |
| 78 | Ron Atkinson | 122 | 2004 FA Cup final |
| 79 | Alex Ferguson | 124 | 2006-07 Season |
| 82 | Viv Anderson | 126 | 2007-08 Season |
| 86 | 1990s | 128 | 2008 Champions League |
| 88 | 1990 FA Cup final v Crystal Palace | 132 | Top ten heaviest defeats |
| 90 | 1992 League Cup final | 134 | 2008 FIFA Club World Cup |
| 92 | 1992-93 Premier League trophy | 136 | 2008-09 League |
| 94 | Eric Cantona | 140 | 2010s |
| 96 | 1994 FA Cup final v Chelsea | 142 | Dimitar Berbatov |
| 98 | 1995-96 Season | 144 | Robin van Persie |
| 100 | All-Time Manchester United Top Goalscorers | 146 | 2012-13 |
| 102 | 1996-97 Season | 148 | 2012-13 Premier League Cup |
| 104 | Andy Cole | 150 | David Moyes |
| 106 | Alex Ferguson | 152 | Louis van Gaal |
| 108 | 1999 FA Cup | 154 | 2014-2015 Wayne Rooney |
| 110 | 1999 Champions League | 156 | 2015-16 Champions League |
| 114 | 2000s | 158 | CSKA Moscow |
| | | 160 | Manchester United Trophy Cabinet |

One of the most successful and iconic teams in the history of the beautiful game, Manchester United is a club which is synonymous with style and flair, boasting an incredible record of winning trophies on the pitch and a global fan base in the millions across the world.

Founded in 1878, the club has won a record 20 English league titles and been crowned the champions of Europe three times, to forge a reputation as one of the greatest clubs football has ever seen. No side has lifted the Premier League trophy more times than United, while their 11 glorious FA Cup triumphs puts the club second on the all-time list of winners of the oldest competition in football.

A fascinating insight into the unique and glittering history of The Red Devils, The Manchester United Story is a stunning pictorial account of the club's birth, remarkable rise to prominence through the decades and, modern dominance of the Old

Trafford side and is essential reading for supporters of the world-famous club everywhere.

From the club's humble beginnings in the late 19th century as Newton Heath, an amateur side formed by local railway workers, to its modern incarnation as a global football phenomenon and giant of the Premier League, The Manchester United Story retraces all the seminal moments of the club's incredible history and salutes the players and managers who've helped make the club the force it is today.

There have, of course, been both lows and highs over the decades since the club's first ever recorded

The 1957 league champions who were involved in the Munich air disaster of February 6th 1958.
Back row: Webster, McGuinness, Blanchflower, Doherty, Colman.
Middle row: Curry, Foulkes, Charlton, Goodwin, Wood, Whelan, Jones, Edwards, Inglis
Front row: Viollet, Berry, Busby, Byrne, Murphy, Taylor, Pegg.

fixture back in 1880, but Manchester United have always greeted victory with humility and adversity with courage. The club is now one of the most famous on the planet, a byword for sporting excellence and entertainment.

United's first major trophy came over a century ago when the side was crowned First Division champions in 1908 and ever since The Red Devils have been relentlessly amassing silverware at home, in Europe and beyond, and the club now proudly boast more top flight titles than any other English side.

The Red Devils were also the first English team ever to lift the European Cup in 1968 and they remain the only English side to have ever been crowned the best club side on the planet, after their triumphs at the Intercontinental Cup in Tokyo in 1999 and the FIFA Club World Cup in Yokohama in 2008.

The last 25 years in particular, have seen United become a side without equal in England and their devastating displays since the start of the Premier League in the 1992-93 season, winning the title in its inaugural year, has cemented the club's place at the very top of the domestic game.

Some of the game's greatest players have pulled on the famous red shirt over the years and from George Best to Cristiano Ronaldo, Charlton and Wayne Rooney, Denis Law to Eric Cantona, The Manchester United Story remembers the stellar contributions made by these iconic players and their team-mates, and how they dazzled successive generations of supporters at the Theatre of Dreams.

Manchester United have also been graced with the services of two of the most successful managers in the history of the beautiful game. The incredible impact made first Sir Matt Busby in the 1950s and 60s and more recently by his fellow Scot Sir Alex Ferguson at Old Trafford are both commemorated, a fitting tribute to two truly visionary coaches who between them presided over more than 2,600 competitive United matches and claimed a magnificent haul of 36 major trophies.

There are many more chapters yet to be written in the remarkable history of The Red Devils and more trophies to be lifted but The Manchester United Story brings to life, decade by decade from the 1880s onwards, all the most memorable moments, pivotal matches and star performances so far.

# THE EARLY YEARS

# 1880s to 1900s

Billy Meredith and Steve Bloomer circa 1900

# THE 1880s

The Manchester United story began in 1878, when employees at the Newton Heath depot of the Lancaster and Yorkshire Railway Company came together to discuss forming a football team. The rail workers wanted a club to call their own and when the company agreed to pay for the lease on a new ground, Newton Heath LYR was born.

It would be another 24 years and the 20th century before the team was renamed, but Newton Heath the club, which was destined to dominate English football, took its first steps in the game.

For the first two years the club played friendly matches against other rail company sides. No reports of those games have survived, but in November 1880 Newton Heath played its first recorded match when they faced the Bolton Wanderers reserve team. Although it ended in a 6-0 defeat, the club was moving forward.

An appearance in the final of the Manchester and District Challenge Cup in 1885 underlined the club's progress, despite losing in the second round. The following year Newton Heath won the competition for the first time, beating Manchester 2-1 in the final at Whalley Range in front of 6000 fans to seal the club's first ever piece of silverware.

In 1886, the team also entered the FA Cup for the first time, falling at the first hurdle to Fleetwood Rangers, but it was in 1888 that a significant new chapter began. The club became one of the 20 founding members of a regional league called The Combination, and the era of the club playing mostly friendly fixtures against local sides was over.

The Combination folded after just one season, but league football was here to stay and Newton Heath joined the 12-team Football Alliance ahead of the 1889-90 campaign. After picking up nine victories in 22 games, and Scottish half-back Willie Stewart top scoring with 10 goals in 19 appearances, the side finished eighth in the final league table.

The first full decade in the club's history was over, and with four triumphs in the Manchester and District Challenge Cup, a first taste of FA Cup action and the switch to league football, Newton Heath were well on their way to bigger and better things.

THE CLUB BECAME ONE OF THE 20 FOUNDING MEMBERS OF A REGIONAL LEAGUE CALLED THE COMBINATION, AND THE ERA OF THE CLUB PLAYING MOSTLY FRIENDLY FIXTURES AGAINST LOCAL SIDES WAS OVER

# THE 1890s

If the 1880s was the decade in which Newton Heath established itself as a force in Manchester, the 1890s was the period when the club began to spread its wings and make a name for itself beyond the confines of the city.

The 1890-91 and 1891-92 seasons saw the team continue to play in the Football Alliance, and it was in the latter campaign that the team enjoyed its best season yet. The team won 12 matches and lost just three times in 22 games to finish second in the table behind champions Nottingham Forest.

It earned the club promotion to the Football League for the first time. Although they eventually finished bottom of the First Division, the team avoided relegation after beating Division Two champions Small Heath, later to become Birmingham City, in a two-legged play-off.

Sadly, another last-placed finish the following season did see Newton Heath relegated after losing their play-off against Liverpool. The club would spend the next 12 years in the second tier of English football.

The decade was far from wasted, though. In January 1894, Newton Heath beat Middlesbrough 4-0 to go through to the second round of the FA Cup for the first time, while in the 1896-97 season wins over Kettering Town and Southampton St. Mary's saw the side reach the third round.

There were big milestones in the club's short history off the pitch, too. In 1892 Alfred Harold Albut, more commonly known as A.H. Albut, was named club secretary, becoming Newton Heath's first ever full-time employee.

## THE FIRST LEAGUE FIXTURE AT BANK STREET, IN SEPTEMBER 1893, SAW NEWTON HEATH HOST BURNLEY IN DIVISION ONE

One of his first tasks was to find the club a new place to play after they were evicted from their original home, North Road, in June 1893. Albut proved just the man for the job when he successfully negotiated the use of the Bank Street ground in the Clayton area of Manchester, overseeing the construction of two new stands to bring the capacity up to 50,000. Bank Street would remain the club's home for the next 17 years, before they moved to the purpose-built Old Trafford.

The first league fixture at Bank Street, in September 1893, saw Newton Heath host Burnley in Division One. The side celebrated the occasion with a 3-2 win over The Clarets, thanks to a hat-trick from English inside right Alf Farnham.

Team pose at Bank Street before the 1905-06 season.
Back row: Downie, Moget, Bonthron,
Middle row: Mangnall, Picken, Sagar, Blackstock, Peddie, Bacon
Front row: Beddow, Roberts, Bell, Arkesden

# THE 1900s

The advent of the 20th century ushered in one of the most exciting decades in Newton Heath's short history and although it began anxiously, with the club teetering on the brink of financial collapse, it ended with the team celebrating their maiden triumphs in both the First Division and the FA Cup.

The money problems reached a head in January 1902 when disgruntled club president William Healey applied for a winding-up order against Heath, claiming he was owed over £240, but a chance meeting between first-team captain Harry

Stafford and a successful brewery owner by the name of John Henry Davies saw the latter agree to pay off Heath's estimated £2,000 debts and the club was dragged back from the precipice.

INCREASINGLY STRONG PERFORMANCES IN THE SECOND DIVISION EVENTUALLY SAW THE SIDE PROMOTED BACK TO DIVISION ONE AT THE END OF THE 1905-06 SEASON.

The rescue deal by Davies and three other benefactors also saw the club embrace a new identity, and after rejecting Manchester Celtic and Manchester Central as possible new names, Newton Heath was rechristened Manchester United.

With the future secured and the appointment of Ernest Mangnall as manager in 1903, United soon began to prosper on the pitch. Increasingly strong performances in the Second Division eventually saw the side promoted back to Division One at the end of the 1905-06 season after they finished runners-up, and within three years The Red Devils had lifted their first two major trophies.

The first was the First Division trophy in 1907-08 as Mangnall's side were crowned league champions for the first time. The side were defeated just nine times in 38 games, beating Aston to the title by a commanding nine point margin, while the star turn for United over the campaign was top scorer Sandy Turnbull with 25 of the team's 81 goals, including hat-tricks against Liverpool, Blackburn Rovers and a four-goal salvo against Arsenal.

A year later the club famously lifted the FA Cup. United claimed the scalps of Brighton & Hove Albion, Everton, Blackburn, Burnley and Newcastle United en route to the final, and in April 1909 they faced Bristol City at Crystal Palace for the right to lift the iconic trophy.

United had failed to beat Bristol in either of the First Division clashes between the two teams earlier in the season, but they emerged victorious from a cagey contest in London which finished 1-0 after a 22nd-minute strike from Turnbull. Some 23 years after they had first entered the competition, United were FA Cup winners.

The 1905-06 campaign was Manchester United's 12 successive season in the second tier of English football and, after more than a decade, the patience of the fans was finally rewarded as their side finished runners-up in Division Two behind Bristol City to earn promotion.

United lost just four of their 38 league fixtures en route to second place, beginning the season with six victories on the bounce before they were held to a goalless draw by Bradford City at Old Trafford in early October, and finished nine points clear of third-placed Chelsea. Eight times during the campaign United scored five or more goals in a single match.

The star turn for The Red Devils was Scottish inside forward Jack Picken, who top-scored for Ernest Magnall's team with 20 league goals and 25 in all competitions. Signed by United in 1905 from Southern League side Plymouth Argyle, Picken topped the scoring charts just once in his six years with The Red Devils but his strikes in 1905-06 will never be forgotten as they were pivotal in propelling the team back into the top flight.

Picken began his prolific season with a goal in a 5-1 victory over Bristol City in early September and after a hat-trick against Chesterfield in March, he signed off with a brace in a 6-0 demolition of Burton United on the last day of the season. Picken left United to play for Burnley in 1911 having scored 39 goals in 113 league appearances for the club.

The 1907-08 season was a major milestone in Manchester United's history as Ernest Mangnall's team became Division One champions, the first of the club's record 20 English top flight titles.

The Red Devils kicked off the campaign in September with a convincing 4-1 victory against Aston Villa and the side underlined their potency in their second fixture, demolishing Liverpool 4-0 at Bank Street. United's free-scoring form continued with a 6-1 mauling of Newcastle United and 5-1 success against

Blackburn Rovers in October and at the end of the campaign, United were the division's top scorers with 81 goals in 38 games. They were involved in just one goalless draw, a stalemate against Preston North End in late December.

It was only the club's 16th season in the embryonic Football League and one in which the side also reached the fourth round of the FA Cup for the first time, eventually losing 2-1 to Fulham at Craven Cottage in March.

Manchester United team pose for photograph with the League Championship trophy in 1908.

Standing: Mangnall, Bacon, Picken, Edmonds, Murray, Moger, Davies, Homer, Lawton, Bell, Deakin

Sitting: Merefith, Duckworth, Roberts, Turnbull, West, Stacey, Whalley, Hofton, Halse, Wall.

Top scorer for the historic season was Scottish forward Sandy Turnbull, who found the back of the net 25 times in the league to help United take significant strides to the silverware. Signed from Manchester City in 1906, Turnbull made a total of 220 appearances for The Red Devils and registered 90 goals.

He scored two hat-tricks during 1907-08 – against Liverpool at Old Trafford in early September and Blackburn Rovers at Ewood Park the following month – and also scored four in one game as United thrashed Arsenal 4-2 at home in November.

# BILLY MEREDITH
## THE WELSH WIZARD

One of a relatively rare group of men to have played for both Manchester clubs, Welshman Billy Meredith signed for United on a free transfer from City in May 1906. Although his Old Trafford career was interrupted by World War One, he would be a Red Devil until 1921.

A stylish outside forward, he formed a potent forward line alongside Jimmy Turnbull, Jimmy Bannister and Sandy Turnbull and with the four in tandem, United stormed to the 1907-08 First Division title, finishing nine points clear of second-placed Aston Villa.

Meredith played in the 1911 FA Charity Shield as United dismantled Swindon Town 8-4 at Stamford Bridge, but when league football was suspended for four seasons due to the war, the Welshman's days with the club were numbered. He did represent The Red Devils again, playing for the club between 1919 and 1921, but he eventually rejoined Manchester City on a free in the summer of 1921. He had made 303 appearances for The Red Devils, scoring 35 goals.

At international level Meredith won 48 caps for Wales between 1895 and 1920, and was a key figure when Wales beat England at Highbury to win the 1920 British Home Championship. His 48 caps were a national record at the time and at the age of 45 years and 229 days when he was selected to face England in 1920, he remains the oldest man to have ever represented the Principality.

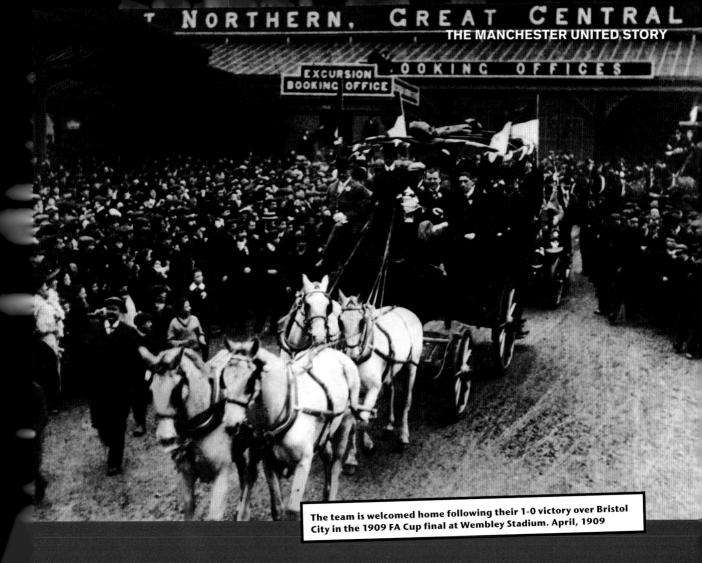

EXCURSION BOOKING OFFICE

OOKING OFFICES

The team is welcomed home following their 1-0 victory over Bristol City in the 1909 FA Cup final at Wembley Stadium. April, 1909

The oldest football competition in the world, the FA Cup has been a happy hunting ground for Manchester United over the years and the club's maiden success famously came in 1909 when they narrowly overcame Bristol City 1-0 at Crystal Palace.

Captained by England centre-half Charlie Roberts, United went into the match having lost to Bristol City in the First Division just a fortnight earlier, but they were able to exact their revenge when Sandy Turnbull was quickest to react to a Harold Halse shot which hit the crossbar, finding the back of the net from the rebound.

The Red Devils found themselves temporarily reduced to 10 men when left back Vince Hayes was injured, but after urgent treatment he was able to return to the action and United were able to resist City's attempted fightback to secure a famous victory.

A crowd of 71,000 crammed into Crystal Palace to witness the club's first ever success in the FA Cup. United had never progressed beyond the fourth round of the competition before but after dispatching Brighton, Everton, Blackburn and Burnley and then Newcastle in the semi-finals, they found themselves on the brink of a maiden triumph.

Turnbull's opportunistic strike ensured United did not waste their golden opportunity to rewrite the record books, while Billy Meredith was named Man of the Match. Jimmy Turnbull top scored for United with five goals in their six FA Cup fixtures, while Sandy Turnbull and Halse were both on target four times over the course of the season.

# 1910s to 1940s

**Len Langford against Norwich. November, 1935**

# THE 1910s

An era inevitably blighted by the tragic events of the First World War, the 1910s saw Manchester United claim a second Division One title but more significantly it was also the decade in which The Red Devils took up permanent residence at their world-famous Old Trafford home.

Designed by famed football stadium architect Archibald Leitch and the estimated construction costs of £60,000 covered by club chairman John Henry Davies, work on Old Trafford had actually begun in 1908 but it was not until February 1910 the new ground was finished and ready to stage its first match.

North West rivals Liverpool were the inaugural visitors to Old Trafford and although a pulsating match ended 4-3 to the Merseysiders, to the disappointment of the majority of the 45,000 strong crowd for the historic fixture, it was not long before the new stadium witnessed a first victory for United as Sheffield United were dispatched in the league at the new ground just a fortnight later.

It was the following year, however, the club's first full season at the stadium, that the love affair between The Red Devils and the ground really blossomed. As United were crowned 1910-11 First Division champions under manager Ernest Mangnall, his side losing just once in their 19 league fixtures at Old Trafford and scoring 47 times over the course of a triumphant campaign.

To further strengthen the growing bond between team and venue, United dramatically clinched the title on the final day of the season with a 5-1 win over Sunderland at Old Trafford, a result which coupled with a defeat for runners-up Aston Villa, handed Mangnall's team the silverware.

Off the pitch, United and Mangnall parted company in 1912 and he was replaced as manager by John Bentley, but his tenure was to be short-lived and after only two years he was in turn replaced by Jack Robson, a football administrator who had served as secretary of Middlesbrough, Crystal Palace and Brighton before his arrival at Old Trafford.

Robson's reign was of course curtailed by the war and in the three full Division One seasons over which he presided either side of hostilities, The Red Devils were unable to finish higher than 12th in the final league table. Pneumonia sadly forced Robson to resign from the job in late 1921 and just a few short months later the illness claimed his life.

TO FURTHER STRENGTHEN THE GROWING BOND BETWEEN TEAM AND VENUE, UNITED DRAMATICALLY CLINCHED THE TITLE ON THE FINAL DAY OF THE SEASON WITH A 5-1 WIN OVER SUNDERLAND AT OLD TRAFFORD

# THE 1920s

A decade to forget from a Manchester United perspective, the 1920s posed problems for The Red Devils both on and off the pitch and while there was no silverware to celebrate, it was a period in the club's history that would make the triumphs that lay ahead all the more satisfying.

It was also a time of significant managerial upheaval, with four different men sitting in the hot seat over the ten years as United searched for a winning formula. They found it, however, only intermittently and for the second time since the club was formed in 1878, United found themselves playing in the second tier of English football.

The decade began with Jack Robson in charge at Old Trafford but he was replaced in late 1921 by Scotsman John Chapman, the former Airdrieonians manager. It was a necessary evil because of Robson's poor health but the change unsettled the team and at the end of the 1921-22 campaign, United were relegated to the Second Division.

They were to spend three years in Division Two before Chapman was able to propel them back up in 1925 and in their first season back in the top flight, The Red Devils finished ninth in the table as well as progressing to the semi-finals of the FA Cup.

Optimism, however, turned to dismay in October 1926 when Chapman was suspended from all football activities by The Football Association for 'improper conduct' and although the FA never elaborated on the exact nature of Chapman's alleged crime, he never worked in football again.

## THEY WERE TO SPEND THREE YEARS IN DIVISION TWO BEFORE CHAPMAN WAS ABLE TO PROPEL THEM BACK UP IN 1925

United wing-half Lal Hilditch stepped into the breach as player-manager until a permanent replacement was found in April the following year. That man was former Oldham, Wigan and Middlesbrough manager Herbert Bamlett and the new boss, as well as the efforts of Hilditch before him, ensured the club did not sacrifice their First Division status, finishing 15th in the table to avoid relegation after what had been a turbulent six months.

Bamlett's three full seasons in the Old Trafford hot seat during the 1920s were in truth a struggle as United came home in 18th, 12th and then 17th in the final standings. Although his side did reach the quarter-finals of the FA Cup in 1928 before going out to Blackburn Rovers, the decade ended with The Red Devils in need of a serious overhaul and an upturn in fortunes.

# THE 1930s

If beleaguered Manchester United fans hoped the 1930s would be more prosperous for their side than the previous decade had proved, they were to be sorely disappointed as the club's woes continued, The Red Devils struggled to keep their heads above water both on and off the pitch.

The alarm bells rang loud and clear as early as 1930 when Herbert Bamlett's side began their 1930-31 Division One campaign with a club record 12 consecutive defeats which included a 6-0 mauling by Huddersfield Town and a 7-4 thrashing by Newcastle United, both in front of the horrified Old Trafford faithful.

The demoralising sequence was finally brought to an end with a 2-0 victory over Birmingham at the start of November but the damage had already been done and United were rock bottom of the table at the end of the season and relegated back to the Second Division for the first time in six years.

Bamlett unsurprisingly tendered his resignation after what had unfolded and was replaced by club secretary Walter Crickmer but he was unable to produce up an immediate reinvigoration of the players and they finished the 1931-32 Division season in midtable obscurity.

At the same time there was worse news in the boardroom as plunging gate receipts threatened to plunge the club into bankruptcy and it was only the last gasp largesse of wealthy manufacturer James Gibson that saved the club when he agreed to invest £30,000.

## THE SENSE OF A NEW START WAS UNDERLINED WITH THE APPOINTMENT OF SCOTT DUNCAN

The sense of a new start was underlined with the appointment of Scott Duncan, a former outside right for Newcastle and Rangers, and although it would take him four frustrating years to get the team back into the top tier of English league football, he finally achieved his goal when United were crowned 1935-36 Division Two champions, beating Charlton to the title by a point.

Sadly, the burgeoning optimism quickly turned to dismay the following season as they were relegated at the first time of asking but a decade of highs and lows continued as The Red Devils recovered from the departure of Duncan in November 1937 but still secured promotion by finishing second under the caretaker stewardship of Crickmer.

The Red Devils' return to the First Division saw the side finish safely if not threateningly in 14th but the following year all thoughts of silverware and glory were forgotten with the outbreak of World War Two and it would be six bloody years before United kicked another ball in anger.

# SCOTT DUNCAN
# 1932-1937

A well-travelled outside right in his playing days, Scott Duncan won the 1908-09 Division One title in England with Newcastle United and also holds the rare distinction of having represented both Rangers and Celtic in his native Scotland.

He turned to football administration and management when he became secretary of Hamilton Academical in 1923 and also filled the same role at Cowdenbeath. He arrived at Old Trafford in turbulent times and although the majority of his reign at the club saw The Red Devils languishing in the second tier, he did preside over their triumphant Second Division title winning campaign in 1935-36 which ended a five-year exile from the top flight.

It was however an epic tussle with Charlton Athletic for the trophy, United recovering from a slow start and four successive defeats in October and November to record a remarkable 19-match unbeaten sequence in the league from January to the end of the campaign which was just enough to overhaul the Addicks.

The two head-to-head meetings between the title rivals saw United emerge 3-0 winners at Old Trafford in September thanks to goals from Tommy Bamford, Jack Cape and Reg Chester while the return game at The Valley just five days later ended in a goalless draw.

Duncan left Manchester United in late 1937 after 223 matches in charge at Old Trafford to become the manager of Ipswich Town. Of those 223 games, United won 88, lost 85 and drew 50 times.

# THE 1940s

The dawn of a new decade signalled a new era at Old Trafford and although it was not until February 1945 that Manchester United were to make their acquaintance with a man who would propel the club to unprecedented new heights, the 1940s was a period in which The Red Devils began in earnest their march to the very top of the football pyramid.

The man to lead United to the promised land was Matt Busby. A former right half for both Manchester City and Liverpool, the Scot had served as a football coach in the Army Physical Training Corps during the War but had no professional management experience when he was named as Walter Crickmer's successor in the Old Trafford hot seat.

The 35-year-old Busby insisted on a five-year contract with the club, arguing he could not instil his methods and playing philosophy on the side overnight, but the Old Trafford faithful did not have to wait that long to realise their new manager was a visionary of real substance.

The 1946-47 season was the first of league football since the end of hostilities and United were a team reborn under Busby, finishing second in Division One and just one point adrift of the champions Liverpool. It was The Red Devils' best finish in the

## THE 1946-47 SEASON WAS THE FIRST OF LEAGUE FOOTBALL SINCE THE END OF HOSTILITIES AND UNITED WERE A TEAM REBORN UNDER BUSBY

top flight since 1911 and a far cry from their pre-War travails in the old Second Division.

Another runners-up finish in the league followed in 1947-48 but any disappointment at missing out on the title was tempered by United's superb run in the FA Cup that season, beating arch rivals Liverpool en route to reaching the final for the first time in 39 years.

Blackpool were the opponents at Wembley in April 1948 and a free scoring encounter finished 4-2 to United courtesy of two goals from Jack Rowley and second-half strikes from Stan Pearson and John Anderson. It was the club's first major trophy since their 1910-11 First Division title and, more importantly, concrete evidence that Busby was the right man to wake the sleeping Manchester giant.

Another second place finish in Division One in 1948-49 behind Portsmouth and an FA Cup semi-final appearance, as well as fourth place in the league the following year, further underlined United's progress and as the 1940s gave way to the 1950s there was a growing sense of anticipation at Old Trafford that more trophies were within touching distance.

# SIR MATT BUSBY
## MANCHESTER UNITED MANAGER 1945-1969

The impact made by Matt Busby at Old Trafford was as immediate as it was prolonged, and from the moment he arrived in the North West in early 1945, Manchester United were a team dramatically transformed.

The Scot was a trailblazer in terms of the remit of the manager, insisting he have control over training, selection and transfers. His methods reaped handsome rewards, as The Red Devils quickly became a real power in the old First Division in the late 1940s, securing three successive runners-up finishes between 1946 and 1949.

Long gone were the days of the side battling relegation each season, and although the club's halcyon era under Busby was to come in the 1950s, the new manager had already shown that United had the potential to become the dominant force in English football.

The 1946-47 campaign under Busby in particular highlighted the progress the team had made under the Scot, United pushing Liverpool all the way for the Division One title. They ultimately came up just one point short, but it was further evidence that The Red Devils were on an upward trajectory, a 5-0 mauling of the Merseysiders at Old Trafford in September courtesy of a Stan Pearson hat-trick the highlight of the season.

The end of the 1940s saw Busby's side maintain their growing consistency with two further second-place finishes, and although they were edged out by Arsenal in the 1948 Charity Shield, Busby ensured the decade did yield silverware in the shape of the 1948 FA Cup.

**1948 FA Cup final at Wembley Stadium.
Manchester United 4 v Blackpool 2**

Manchester United's triumph over Blackpool in the 1948 FA Cup final was a cathartic experience for the club after two decades of underachievement, and in front of 100,000 spectators at Wembley, The Red Devils produced a captivating display of attacking football which swept aside The Tangerines.

United's path to the final had been a tough one. Drawn against Liverpool in the fourth round, a 3-0 victory over their old rivals at Old Trafford provided the catalyst for a dominant run in which they beat Charlton, Preston North End and Derby County in the semi-final to book their place at Wembley.

Captained by Ireland full-back Johnny Carey in the final, United recovered from going behind in the 12th minute with a Jack Rowley equaliser, but were 2-1 in arrears at half-time after a Stan Mortensen strike for Blackpool. The second half, however, was an altogether different story as Matt Busby's side charged forward, Rowley levelling up in the 70th minute before Stan Pearson and then John Anderson supplied the coup de grace to settle the match 4-2 and hand United the FA Cup for the first time since 1909. It was also the team's first major silverware since they had been crowned First Division champions 37 years earlier.

Busby's side scored 22 times in six FA Cup fixtures in 1947-48, with Pearson leading the way with eight goals and Rowley on target five times.

# 1950s

Manchester United v Arsenal in league match.
Final score Manchester United 6-1 Arsenal. April, 1952

# THE 1950s

A tumultuous decade in the history of Manchester United, the 1950s brought triumph and tragedy to the club in equal measure. Although the team's three First Division titles in the space of six seasons will never be forgotten, the catastrophic events of the Munich Air Disaster linger equally long in the memory of The Red Devils faithful.

Runners-up to Tottenham Hotspur in 1950-51, United embarked on the 1951-52 campaign desperate to turn their obvious potential into tangible silverware and after 42 league games, 23 victories and an impressive haul of 95 goals, Busby's side successfully dethroned Spurs to become the champions of England for the first time since 1911.

The next three seasons saw United marginally off the pace in terms of competing for the title, finishing eighth, fourth and fifth respectively, but Busby's troops rallied magnificently between 1955 and 1957 to claim back-to-back Division One crowns, reach a European Cup semi-final and agonisingly miss out on the fabled league and FA Cup double.

The 1955-56 season saw no-one able to stop the United juggernaut as The Red Devils claimed the title by 11 clear points from Blackpool. Their successful defence of the crown the following season was almost as emphatic, finishing eight points ahead of runners-up Tottenham Hotspur and had United not narrowly lost to Aston Villa in the FA Cup final at Wembley at the end of the season, the side would have completed their first ever double.

The celebratory atmosphere which engulfed Old Trafford after their hat-trick of league triumphs was cruelly shattered in February 1958, when the plane carrying the United team back from a European

## THE 1955-56 SEASON SAW NO-ONE ABLE TO STOP THE UNITED JUGGERNAUT AS THE RED DEVILS CLAIMED THE TITLE BY 11 CLEAR POINTS FROM BLACKPOOL

Cup game against Red Star Belgrade crashed in icy conditions on the runway at Munich airport and tragically claimed the lives of 23 of the 40 people on board.

Eight of the United squad, who had been affectionately dubbed the 'Busby Babes', died that day. They were Geoff Bent, Roger Byrne, Eddie Colman, Duncan Edwards, Mark Jones, David Pegg, Tommy Taylor and Billy Whelan, while three club officials, including former manager Walter Crickmer, were also killed in Germany.

Busby himself was seriously injured but recovered after nine weeks in intensive care. He would continue to manage the team for another 11 years but football for once was a secondary consideration in the immediate aftermath of the crash as United remembered those who had been lost.

# FIRST DIVISION

|  | P | W | D | L | F | A | PTS | POS |
|---|---|---|---|---|---|---|---|---|
| 1949-50 | 42 | 18 | 14 | 10 | 69 | 44 | 50 | 4th |
| 1950-51 | 42 | 24 | 8 | 10 | 74 | 40 | 56 | 2nd |
| 1951-52 | 42 | 23 | 11 | 8 | 95 | 52 | 57 | 1st |
| 1952-53 | 42 | 18 | 10 | 14 | 69 | 72 | 46 | 8th |
| 1953-54 | 42 | 18 | 12 | 12 | 73 | 58 | 48 | 4th |
| 1954-55 | 42 | 20 | 7 | 15 | 84 | 74 | 47 | 5th |
| 1955-56 | 42 | 25 | 10 | 7 | 83 | 51 | 60 | 1st |
| 1956-57 | 42 | 28 | 8 | 6 | 103 | 54 | 64 | 1st |
| 1957-58 | 42 | 16 | 11 | 15 | 85 | 75 | 43 | 9th |
| 1958-59 | 42 | 24 | 7 | 11 | 103 | 66 | 55 | 2nd |

# HONOURS

**First Division** 1951-52, 1955-56, 1956-57

**Charity Shield** 1952, 1956, 1957

The 1951-52 season was the real turning point in Matt Busby's reign as Manchester United manager. Four second-place finishes since his appointment were encouraging, as was his side's 1948 FA Cup win, but The Red Devils' ultimate ambition was to be champions again.

The campaign became a massive three-way battle between United, Spurs and Arsenal for the title, but Busby's side held their nerve when it really mattered. They went the last six games unbeaten, which included a 4-0 win over Liverpool at Old Trafford, a 3-0 win over Chelsea and a 6-1 thrashing of The Gunners on the final day. That season, United scored 95 goals in their 42 league games at an average of well over two per game, with only Newcastle scoring more.

United's triumph owed much to the form of Jack Rowley, who was top scorer for The Red Devils with 30 league strikes. Signed from Bournemouth in 1937 for £3000, Rowley hit 182 league goals for United in 380 appearances, but the 1951-52 season was easily his best in a United shirt.

He began the campaign with a hat-trick in the opening game against West Bromwich Albion at The Hawthorns and never looked back, scoring further trebles in wins against Middlesbrough the following weekend, Stoke in September and Arsenal in April.

His total of 211 goals in 424 games in all competitions leaves Rowley fourth on the all-time list of goalscorers for the club.

# DUNCAN EDWARDS

Possibly the most famous of the 'Busby Babes' who lost their lives in the Munich air disaster was Duncan Edwards. The defensive midfielder was just 21 years old when he died, but despite his short life he made a massive impact for both club and country.

Born in Dudley, Worcestershire, Edwards began his love affair with The Red Devils when he joined the club's youth side as a teenager. It wasn't long before he forced his way into the senior reckoning, making his first-team debut in the First Division against Cardiff City in April 1953 at the age of just 16 years and 185 days. At the time, he was the youngest ever player in the top flight of English football.

He quickly became a first-team regular, and was a key part of the Busby side that won back-to-back Division One titles between 1955 and 1957.

Edwards enjoyed only four full seasons at Old Trafford, but in that time amassed more than 177 appearances for the club, scoring 21 times.

His England caps career was equally remarkable, making his international debut against Scotland in April 1955 in the British Home Championship. At 18 years and 183 days, he also become the youngest player to represent The Three Lions since the Second World War. Edwards won a total of 18 England, and scored three goals in six appearances during the 1956-57 season.

EDWARDS ENJOYED ONLY FOUR FULL SEASONS AT OLD TRAFFORD, BUT IN THAT TIME AMASSED MORE THAN 177 APPEARANCES FOR THE CLUB, SCORING 21 TIMES

English League Division One match at Old Trafford. Manchester United 1 v Bolton Wanderers 1. January, 1955

# ALL-TIME TOP APPEARANCES

1

2

4

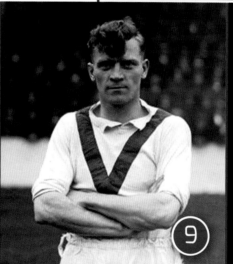

## Appearances

1. Ryan Giggs = 963
2. Sir Bobby Charlton = 758
3. Paul Scholes = 718
4. Bill Foulkes = 688
5. Gary Neville = 602

6. Alex Stepney = 539
7. Tony Dunne = 535
8. Denis Irwin = 529
9. Joe Spence = 510
10. Wayne Rooney = 499

# 1955-56 DIVISION ONE TROPHY

The 1955-56 season brought Manchester United a fourth First Division success in the club's history. Despite a slow start to the campaign, it quickly became a one-horse race as Matt Busby's side strolled to the title, finishing 11 points ahead of second-placed Blackpool.

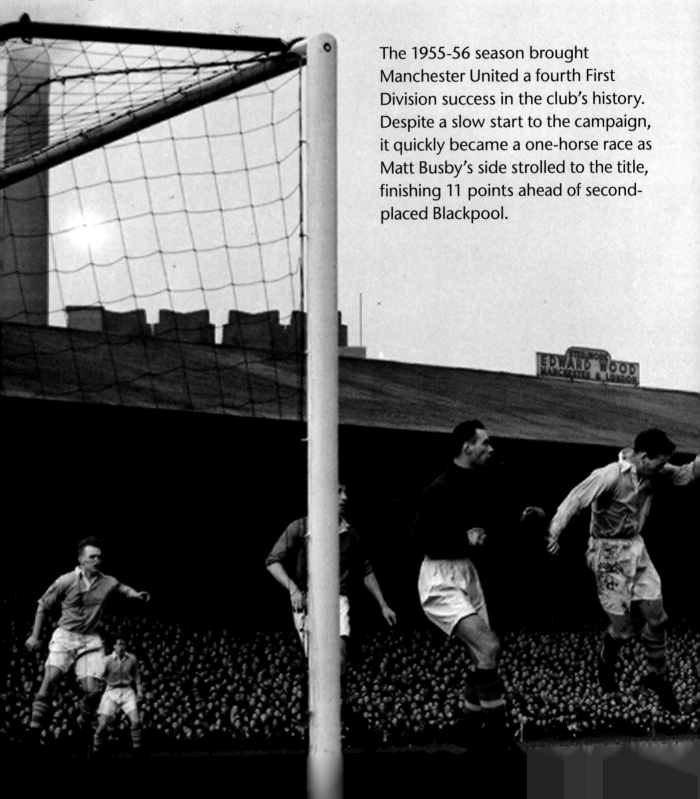

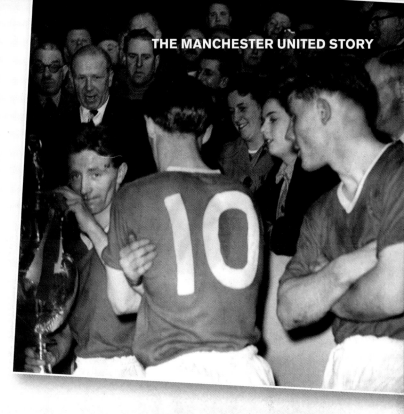

The silverware was effectively sealed with a sensational run of form in the New Year as The Red Devils strung together a run of 14 games between January and late April without defeat. The sequence featured ten wins, including a 2-1 win over Blackpool at Old Trafford, and the chasing pack could find no answer.

United's performances at home over the course of the campaign were excellent, winning 18 of 21 games. The other three matches were drawn, meaning United went the season unbeaten at Old Trafford.

Tommy Taylor top-scored with 25 of the team's 83 league goals, but club legend Dennis Viollet chipped in with 20 in 35 appearances, including a hat-trick in a 4-1 win against West Bromwich Albion on Christmas Eve.

Viollet spent six more seasons at Old Trafford, and the Mancunian's 179 career goals for the club puts him level with George Best as the fifth highest scorer ever in the history of The Red Devils.

UNITED'S PERFORMANCES AT HOME OVER THE COURSE OF THE CAMPAIGN WERE EXCELLENT, WINNING 18 OF 21 GAMES ON THE RIGHT HAND SIDE OF THE BALL

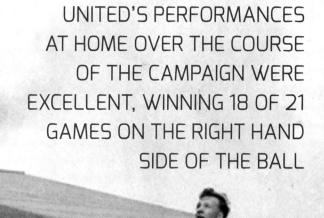

# 1956-57
# DIVISION ONE TROPHY

Manchester United's 1955-56 league win was the club's fourth top flight title, but they had never successfully defended a First Division crown until 1956-57.

UNITED PLAYED 21 TIMES AWAY FROM HOME, WINNING 14 GAMES. THEY DREW FOUR GAMES AND WERE BEATEN JUST THREE TIMES, SCORING MORE GOALS AND CONCEDING FEWER IN AWAY FIXTURES THAN ANY OF THEIR RIVALS

The previous season had seen The Red Devils go unbeaten at Old Trafford, and while they remained a force to be reckoned with at home the following season, it was their powerful displays on the road in 1956-57 which set them apart from the rest of the division.

United played 21 times away from home, winning 14. They drew four games and were beaten just three times, scoring more goals and conceding fewer in away fixtures than any of their rivals.

The team's closest rivals were Tottenham Hotspur, but both fixtures between the two ended in draws. The London side were unable to overhaul United and Busby's team finished eight points clear.

The Red Devils scored a phenomenal 103 league goals during the season, with Ireland international inside forward Billy Whelan finishing as top scorer with 26 strikes.

Like seven of his Old Trafford team-mates, Whelan lost his life in the Munich air disaster. He only ever played for United in his career and boasted a remarkable strike rate in his time with The Red Devils, scoring 43 times in just 79 appearances.

**Tommy Taylor circa 1957**

**Charlton v Manchester United- Bobby Charlton scores first goal for the team. February, 1957**

# TOMMY TAYLOR

As well as claiming a hat-trick of First Division titles in the 1950s, Manchester United also won the Charity Shield three times in the decade, the third of which was in 1957 after a crushing 4-0 victory over Aston Villa at Old Trafford.

The Man of the Match was England centre forward Tommy Taylor, who registered a hat-trick in the match, with outside right Johnny Berry adding the fourth from the penalty spot as United cut loose in front of a crowd of over 28,000.

Taylor had already scored six times in the First Division that season before the Charity Shield in October, and continued his red-hot form against the winners of the 1958 FA Cup with a three-goal haul which Villa had no answer to.

Taylor was to tragically lose his life in Munich the following year at the age of 26, but his incredible strike rate of 131 goals in just 191 appearances for the club is testament to his talent.

The Charity Shield triumph proved to be the highlight of United's season as Busby's team finished a distant ninth in the First Division table and were beaten 2-0 by Bolton Wanderers in the FA Cup Final. They did reach the semi-finals in the European Cup, but hope turned to heartbreak against AC Milan as The Red Devils won the first leg 2-1, only to lose the return match 4-0.

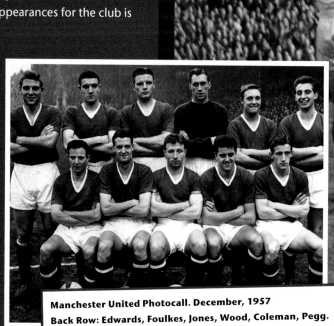

Manchester United Photocall. December, 1957
Back Row: Edwards, Foulkes, Jones, Wood, Coleman, Pegg.
Front Row: Berry, Whelan, Taylor, Viollet

# 1960s

Manchester United v Leicester City. 1963 FA Cup final at Wembley Stadium.
Matt Busby leads out the team.

# THE 1960s

The start of the 1960s saw all those associated with Manchester United slowly coming to terms with the aftermath of the Munich air crash. Although the loss of 11 club employees would never be forgotten, Matt Busby was determined to focus on matters on the pitch and the renewed pursuit of silverware as he rebuilt his squad.

It was to be a hugely successful decade, and although United initially failed to make an impact on the First Division, there was another addition to the Old Trafford trophy cabinet in 1963 when Busby's Babes beat Leicester City 3-1 in the FA Cup final.

The side's Wembley triumph proved to be the start of a dramatic upturn in fortunes in the league. After finishing runners-up to Liverpool in 1963-64, they were champions of England for a sixth time in 1964-65, edging out Leeds United on goal difference after both sides had finished level on 61 points.

Six First Division titles became seven in 1966-67, but having reached three European Cup semi-finals under Busby, United's attentions turned once again to the continent and another crack at being crowned the best side in Europe.

No English side had lifted the European Cup since it began in 1955, but that all finally changed in 1968. Scottish side Hibernian were dispatched in the first round, while Bosnian club FK Sarajevo and Gornik Zabrze from Poland were beaten in the second round and quarter-finals respectively. Six-time winners Real Madrid were the opponents in the last four, but United continued their progress thanks to a 4-3 aggregate victory and went on to face Benfica in the final at Wembley.

AFTER FINISHING RUNNERS-UP TO LIVERPOOL IN 1963-64, THEY WERE CHAMPIONS OF ENGLAND FOR A SIXTH TIME IN 1964-65, EDGING OUT LEEDS UNITED ON GOAL DIFFERENCE AFTER BOTH SIDES HAD FINISHED LEVEL ON 61 POINTS

There were no goals in the first 45 minutes, but an incredible second-half performance from United and a famous brace from Bobby Charlton, coupled with goals from George Best and Brian Kidd in extra-time, sealed a historic 4-1 win for Busby's team.

It was United's last piece of silverware of the decade, but United had finally conquered Europe. Although Busby's Old Trafford CV was already glittering, his success in the 1968 European Cup final confirmed the Scot as one football's undisputed all-time greatest managers.

# FIRST DIVISION

| | P | W | D | L | F | A | PTS | POS |
|---|---|---|---|---|---|---|---|---|
| 1959-60 | 42 | 19 | 7 | 16 | 102 | 80 | 45 | 7th |
| 1960-61 | 42 | 18 | 9 | 15 | 88 | 76 | 45 | 7th |
| 1961-62 | 42 | 15 | 9 | 18 | 72 | 75 | 39 | 15th |
| 1962-63 | 42 | 12 | 10 | 20 | 67 | 81 | 34 | 19th |
| 1963-64 | 42 | 23 | 7 | 12 | 90 | 62 | 53 | 2nd |
| 1964-65 | 42 | 26 | 9 | 7 | 89 | 39 | 61 | 1st |
| 1965-66 | 42 | 18 | 15 | 9 | 84 | 59 | 51 | 4th |
| 1966-67 | 42 | 24 | 12 | 6 | 84 | 45 | 60 | 1st |
| 1967-68 | 42 | 24 | 8 | 10 | 89 | 55 | 56 | 2nd |
| 1968-69 | 42 | 15 | 12 | 15 | 57 | 53 | 42 | 11th |

# HONOURS

**First Division** 1964-65, 1966-67

**FA Cup** 1963

**European Cup** 1968

**Charity Shield** 1965, 1967

# 1963
# FA CUP

Their third success in the world's oldest football competition, Manchester United's victory in the 1963 FA Cup final was also the second and last time Matt Busby lifted the trophy during his long and illustrious Old Trafford career.

The Red Devils' march to the final saw Busby's team beat Huddersfield, Aston Villa and Chelsea in the early rounds. After defeating Coventry City in the last eight, a Denis Law strike in the semi-final against Southampton was enough to book the team's place at Wembley and a meeting with Leicester City.

United had failed to beat The Foxes home or away in league action that season but they turned the tables on Leicester at Wembley, taking a 30th minute lead through Law.

Scotland forward David Herd doubled The Red Devils' advantage 12 minutes into the second half and although Leicester gave themselves a chance with a goal ten minutes from time, Busby's team wrapped up a 3-1 victory when Herd pounced for his second late on.

Six of the United squad played in all six FA Cup games that year. They were England centre-back Bill Foulkes, wing back Maurice Setters, Bobby Charlton, Republic of Ireland midfielder Johnny Giles, Law and fellow Scot Herd. Law was also United's top scorer in the competition that season with six, including a hat-trick in the 5-0 demolition of Huddersfield in the third round.

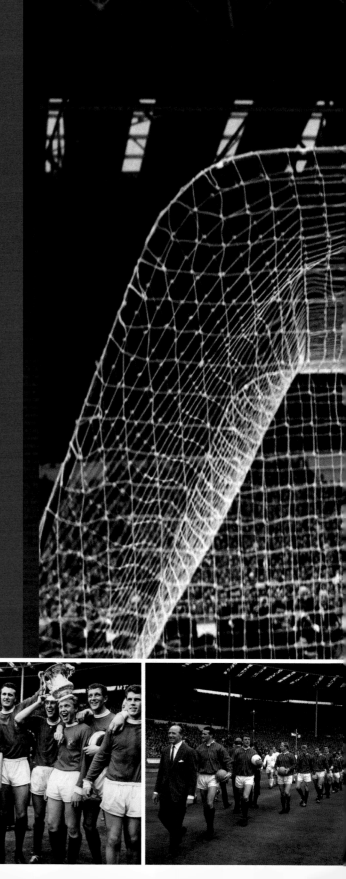

THE RED DEVILS' MARCH TO THE
FINAL SAW BUSBY'S TEAM BEAT
HUDDERSFIELD, ASTON VILLA AND
CHELSEA IN THE EARLY ROUNDS

**FA Cup final at Wembley Stadium.
Manchester United 3 v Leicester City 1. May, 1963**

# DENIS LAW

Signed from Italian side Torino in 1962 for a then British record fee of £115,000, Denis Law spent 11 fantastic years at Old Trafford. Only Sir Bobby Charlton and Wayne Rooney have scored more than the Scottish centre forward's 237 goals for the club in 404 appearances in the famous red shirt.

One of Law's finest seasons came in 1964-65, when he top-scored for the club for a third successive year. He netted 28 times in 36 Division One games to help secure the title for The Red Devils for the first time in eight years.

This included a stunning four-goal display in a 7-0 demolition of Aston Villa in late October, while the magical striker bagged a brace seven times during the course of the season. He netted crucial doubles in April in a 3-0 defeat of Liverpool and again two days later in a 3-1 win over Arsenal at Old Trafford, which effectively sealed the silverware for United ahead of Leeds United.

The forward scored 39 goals in total in all competitions in 1964-65, scoring eight in 10 appearances in the team's progress to the semi-finals of the Inter-Cities Fairs Cup and three times in six FA Cup fixtures as Busby's side made it through to the semi-final.

His most prolific ever season for The Red Devils had actually come the year before, when he netted 46 times in just 42 games, but his goals in 1964-65 were crucial in United's title win.

**Nottingham Forest 2 v Manchester United 2. Denis Law returns from suspension to slam home two goals. January, 1965**

# 1964-65 DIVISION ONE TROPHY

A thrilling 1964-65 season saw Manchester United and Leeds United fight out an epic title scrap. It was neck-and-neck during the campaign, but the turning point came in April when The Red Devils crossed the Pennines to face Leeds at Elland Road and snatched a 1-0 victory thanks to a John Connelly goal.

The result proved crucial as Matt Busby's side won six points from a possible eight in their four remaining Division One games, while Leeds' form slumped, managing only two victories in their last four matches.

Both teams ended the season level on 61 points after 42 games but United's massively superior goal difference – plus 50 in comparison to Leeds' plus 31 – was key. United hit 89 league goals for the season, but it was the team's defence that really cemented their position as the best side in the division, conceding less than a goal a game during the season.

The leading lights of The Red Devils' brilliant defence were Republic of Ireland full-backs Shay Brennan and Tony Dunne, and English centre-back Bill Foulkes. The three started all 42 First Division games for United, while Ireland goalkeeper Pat Dunne featured 37 times in the league. The only other ever present under Busby that season was outside forward John Connelly, who also chipped in with 15 goals.

> UNITED HIT 89 LEAGUE GOALS FOR THE SEASON, BUT IT WAS THE TEAM'S DEFENCE THAT REALLY CEMENTED THEIR POSITION AS THE BEST SIDE IN THE DIVISION

# GEORGE BEST

One of the greatest talents ever to have graced Old Trafford, George Best was an ever present for the club during the 1966-67 season as Manchester United were crowned league champions for the seventh time in their history.

The magical Northern Ireland star began the campaign with a bang, scoring on the opening weekend against West Bromwich Albion. But arguably his best display came in December, when he was on target twice in a 2-2 draw with arch-rivals Liverpool at Old Trafford. His final goal of the campaign came in May in a 6-1 demolition of West Ham United at Upton Park.

The Red Devils were Division One's top scorers in 1966-67 with 84, and the attacking trio of Best, Denis Law and Bobby Charlton accounted for more than half the team's total as Busby's side finished four points clear of Nottingham Forest and Tottenham Hotspur.

Best's United career lasted 11 amazing seasons. During that time, he claimed two First Division winner's medals and the European Cup. In total, he scored 179 goals in 470 appearances in all competitions, leaving him joint fifth on the all-time goals list alongside Dennis Viollet.

At international level, the Belfast-born attacking midfielder represented Northern Ireland 37 times between 1964 and 1977, scoring nine times, and although he never played in a World Cup or European Championship finals, he is still easily the country's most famous player.

**George Best for Manchester United circa 1967**

"GEORGE BEST WAS THE GREATEST PLAYER IN THE WORLD."

PELE

# 1966-67 DIVISION ONE TROPHY

Manchester United's title win in 1966-67 was the fifth and final league win of the Matt Busby reign at Old Trafford, and the seventh time The Red Devils had been crowned the champions of England.

The battle for silverware was a tight four-way battle between United, Nottingham Forest, Spurs and Leeds United, and although just four points separated them at the end of the season, United won thanks to an amazing climax to their league campaign.

A 2-1 defeat to Sheffield United at Bramall Lane on Boxing Day was their sixth and last of the season, going on a stunning 21-game unbeaten streak that ultimately got the team over the winning line ahead of their title rivals.

United's form at Old Trafford in particular was irresistible, winning 17 and drawing four of their 21 league games there. Four United players reached double figures in the First Division for the season as Dennis Law (23), David Herd (16), Bobby Charlton (12) and George Best (10) helped The Red Devils score 84 goals, more than any other side in the division.

The 1966-67 season also saw the return of Manchester City to the top flight after a three-year absence. United welcomed their city neighbours back to the division with a 1-0 victory at Old Trafford in September, thanks to a goal from Law, while the rematch at Maine Road in January finished 1-1.

# BOBBY CHARLTON V BENFICA

## 1968 EUROPEAN CUP

Manchester United's famous 4-1 victory over Benfica in the final of the 1968 European Cup was the dawn of a new era for the club as they claimed their first piece of European silverware.

Bobby Charlton's second-half header gave United the lead in front of a crowd of more than 92,000 at Wembley, but his effort was cancelled out by a late Benfica equaliser with 11 minutes left to take the final into extra-time.

It was Matt Busby's side that proved stronger in the additional 30 minutes of play. They stormed to a landmark win courtesy of a sublime solo dribble and finish from George Best just two

minutes into extra-time, a powerful header from Brian Kidd, two minutes later who was celebrating his 19th birthday that day, and an unstoppable near-post drive from Charlton.

Charlton's strikes at the home of English football were two of the 22 goals he scored for the club in Europe in 45 appearances during his 17 seasons as a Red Devil. In total, the legendary midfielder scored 249 goals in 748 games in all competitions between 1956 and 1973 to seal his place in folklore as one of the greatest ever players to represent United. He helped the club win three Division One titles, the FA Cup and the European Cup, and also won over a century of England caps.

# UNITED

# EUROPEAN CUP

Manchester United have been crowned champions of Europe three times in their illustrious history, and the club's love affair with continental football began after that European Cup victory over two-time champions Benfica.

Playing in unfamiliar blue shirts, Matt Busby's team were hoping to emulate Celtic's success in the final 12 months earlier when they became the first British champions. In front of a Wembley crowd of 92,225, United ensured that in the 13th year of the competition, an English club's name would finally be engraved on the trophy.

It proved to be a roller-coaster encounter as the European Cup was decided in extra-time for only the second time in its history, but The Red Devils were eventually victorious over their Portuguese opponents.

It would be another 31 years before United again experienced the unique atmosphere of the biggest club game in world football, but success in 1968 further underlined their status as one of the heavyweights of European football. United's victory at Wembley also brought the last silverware of Busby's glittering career as Old Trafford manager, and although he would remain at the helm for one more season, it was a suitably triumphant note for the great man's sign-off.

**The team with the European Cup at Old Trafford. July, 1968**

**L-R Top-Bottom: Foulkes, Aston, Rimmer, Stepney, Gowling, Herd, Sadler, Dunne, Brannan, Crerand, Best, Burns, Crompton, Ryan, Stiles, Law, Busby, Charlton, Kidd, Fitzpatrick**

IT PROVED TO BE A ROLLER-COASTER ENCOUNTER
AS THE EUROPEAN CUP WAS DECIDED IN EXTRA-TIME
FOR ONLY THE SECOND TIME IN ITS HISTORY, BUT THE
RED DEVILS WERE EVENTUALLY VICTORIOUS OVER
THEIR PORTUGUESE OPPONENTS

# RED DEVILS
# TOP TEN HOME WINS

②

1. Manchester United 10-0 Anderlecht, Sep 1956

2. Manchester United 6-0 Newcastle United, Jan 2008

3. Manchester United 7-1 Roma, April 2007

4. Manchester United 7-1 Blackburn Rovers, Nov 2010

5. Manchester United 6-1 Liverpool, Sep 1928

6. Manchester United 7-0 Barnsley, Oct 1997

7. Manchester United 8-0 Yeovil Town, Feb 1949

8. Manchester United 8-1 Queens Park Rangers, March 1969

9. Manchester United 9-0 Ipswich Town, March 1995

10. Manchester United 8-2 Arsenal, Aug 2011

# 1970s

1977 FA Cup final- Liverpool v Manchester United. Jimmy and Brian Greenhoff hold the FA Cup after beating Liverpool 2-1.

# THE 1970s

Although Manchester United were to claim a fourth FA Cup and another Charity Shield in the 1970s, the decade saw massive managerial upheaval at Old Trafford. A total of five mangers were to take charge of the first team as the club's search for new momentum in the post-Busby era proved beyond them.

The decade began with Mancunian Wilf McGuinness in charge. He was just 31 when he was named Matt Busby's successor in the summer of 1969, but his inexperience saw him struggle to fill Busby's sizeable shoes, and in December 1970 he was sacked by the club, going back to his previous role as reserve team manager. Busby briefly came out of retirement to hold the fort to the end of the 1970-71 season.

A permanent replacement was found in the shape of Frank O'Farrell but the Irishman, who had just steered Leicester City to promotion from Division Two, endured a nightmare 18 months in charge before he too was sacked.

The next man in the hot-seat was Tommy Docherty. United persuaded Docherty to give up his role as Scotland manager to come to Old Trafford, but despite steering the team to a famous victory over Liverpool in the 1977 FA Cup final during his five years in charge, the Scot was also responsible for The Red Devils' relegation to the Second Division at the end of the 1973-74 season.

United, however, kept faith with Docherty after the disappointment of relegation, and he repaid the club at the first time of asking, guiding the team to the Division Two title and an immediate return to the top flight.

The next two First Division campaigns under Docherty saw the team finish third and sixth respectively, but just two months after he masterminded United's triumph over Liverpool at Wembley, he found himself out of a job.

The club turned to Queens Park Rangers manager Dave Sexton to take charge. Sexton was seen as a safe pair of hands in the wake of Docherty's reign, but safety didn't signify silverware and although United did share the 1977 Charity Shield with Liverpool, the decade would end with no further additions to the trophy cabinet.

There were close calls – United finished runners-up to Arsenal in the FA Cup final in 1979 and Liverpool in the league in 1979-80 – but they were unable to recapture the spark that had swept them to such success in the two previous decades.

UNITED FINISHED RUNNERS-UP TO ARSENAL IN THE FA CUP FINAL IN 1979 AND LIVERPOOL IN THE LEAGUE IN 1979-80 - BUT THEY WERE UNABLE TO RECAPTURE THE SPARK THAT HAD SWEPT THEM TO SUCH SUCCESS IN THE TWO PREVIOUS DECADES

# FIRST DIVISION

|  | P | W | D | L | F | A | PTS | POS |
|---|---|---|---|---|---|---|---|---|
| 1969-70 | 42 | 14 | 17 | 11 | 66 | 61 | 45 | 8th |
| 1970-71 | 42 | 16 | 11 | 15 | 65 | 66 | 43 | 8th |
| 1971-72 | 42 | 19 | 10 | 13 | 69 | 61 | 48 | 8th |
| 1972-73 | 42 | 12 | 13 | 17 | 44 | 60 | 37 | 18th |
| 1973-74 | 42 | 10 | 12 | 20 | 38 | 48 | 32 | 21st |

# SECOND DIVISION

|  | P | W | D | L | F | A | PTS | POS |
|---|---|---|---|---|---|---|---|---|
| 1974-75 | 42 | 26 | 9 | 7 | 66 | 30 | 61 | 1st |

# FIRST DIVISION

|  | P | W | D | L | F | A | PTS | POS |
|---|---|---|---|---|---|---|---|---|
| 1975-76 | 42 | 23 | 10 | 9 | 68 | 42 | 56 | 3rd |
| 1976-77 | 42 | 18 | 11 | 13 | 71 | 62 | 47 | 6th |
| 1977-78 | 42 | 16 | 10 | 16 | 67 | 63 | 42 | 10th |
| 1978-79 | 42 | 15 | 15 | 12 | 60 | 63 | 45 | 9th |

# HONOURS

**Second Division** 1974-75

**FA Cup** 1977

**Charity Shield** 1977

# MANAGER PROFILES

## WILF McGUINNESS, MATT BUSBY AND FRANK O'FARRELL

The start of the 1970s saw Manchester United managed by three different men in the space of just two years and although the decade began with Wilf McGuinness in charge, he was sacked in December 1970 after his side had registered just five victories in their opening 23 Division One fixtures of the season.

The club's decision to dispense with McGuinness' services prompted Matt Busby to dust off his tracksuit one last time and come out of retirement at the age of 61 to take charge of the team until the end of the 1970-71 season. The legendary Scot duly guided United safely home in eighth place in the First Division and to the semi-finals of the FA Cup, and although there some sentimental supporters who wanted to Busby to return for the following year, he stepped aside as arranged at the end of the season.

The appointment of Frank O'Farrell as the club's new manager in 1971 proved to be ultimately ill-fated, and although the Irishman successfully emulated Busby's eighth-place finish in his first full season with the club, United's form dipped alarmingly the following year.

The Red Devils failed to win any of their first nine league matches in the 1972-73 season and although there was a minor revival, a 5-0 humiliation against Crystal Palace at Selhurst Park in December made it just five wins in 22 games. It was the final straw for the United board and O'Farrell was sacked after only 81 games in the hot seat.

Ipswich Town 0 v Manchester United 1. Wilf McGuinness calls off injured Morgan. January, 1970

Bobby Charlton chased in the street by children of Dounside Purley School in Surrey. Watched by Sir Matt Busby and Derek Dougan. November, 1970

Frank O'Farrell. August, 1971

> "I NEVER WANTED MANCHESTER UNITED TO BE SECOND TO ANYBODY. ONLY THE BEST WOULD BE GOOD ENOUGH."
> SIR MATT BUSBY

Frank O'Farrell and Sir Matt Busby. July, 1971

Wilf McGuinness and Sir Matt Busby. April, 1969

Wilf McGuinness. February, 1969

# TOMMY DOCHERTY
## NEW UNITED MANAGER 1972

Manchester United pulled off something of a coup in 1972 when they unveiled Tommy Docherty as their new manager, convincing the then 44-year-old to leave his job as Scotland manager to replace Frank O'Farrell at Old Trafford. His reign was rarely dull, and although he was the man who took The Red Devils down to the Second Division in 1975, he made up for it by bringing the team straight back up and winning the 1977 FA Cup against arch-rivals Liverpool.

As a player, Docherty made his name as a right-half with Preston North End, Arsenal and Scotland, and by the time he had arrived at Old Trafford, just three days before Christmas, he had already enjoyed managerial stints with Chelsea, Rotherham United, Queens Park Rangers, Aston Villa and Porto.

United avoided relegation in 1972-73 after Docherty's arrival in December, but it could not be escaped the following season. The exile from the top-flight was short-lived, while the side's FA Cup success ended a 14-year wait to lift the famous old trophy.

The side's third-place finish in 1975-76 suggested Docherty was making real progress in the league, but a year later he left Old Trafford. The Scot was in charge for a total of 215 games, registering 99 victories, 62 defeats and 54 draws over five years.

Tommy Docherty with players Denis Law and David Sadler after their league division one match against Leeds United at Old Trafford. December, 1972.

# 1973-74

The 1973-74 campaign was a disaster for The Red Devils. It marked the last time the club suffered relegation to the second tier of English football after a season in which they only won ten out of their 42 matches.

A lack of goals – 38 in total – proved their downfall, with Northern Ireland midfielder Sammy McIlroy top scorer the league with just six as the team finished five points from safety.

Two wins in their opening three First Division fixtures filled the Old Trafford faithful with hope at the start of the campaign, but a run of nine league games without a win in November and December set the alarm bells ringing. After an eight-match sequence in the New Year in which the side failed to register a victory, the writing was on the wall for United.

There was still hope of avoiding the drop as late as April, but three successive 1-0 defeats to Everton, Manchester City and Stoke in the team's final three games put paid to hopes of completing a great escape and The Red Devils finished in 21st in the table, three points above bottom club Norwich City.

There was little joy for the United faithful in the season's cup competitions, either. The team were knocked out of the FA Cup in the fourth round after a 1-0 defeat to Ipswich Town, and the League Cup at the first hurdle after another 1-0 loss, this time against Middlesbrough.

## TWO WINS IN THEIR OPENING THREE FIRST DIVISION FIXTURES FILLED THE OLD TRAFFORD FAITHFUL WITH HOPE AT THE START OF THE CAMPAIGN

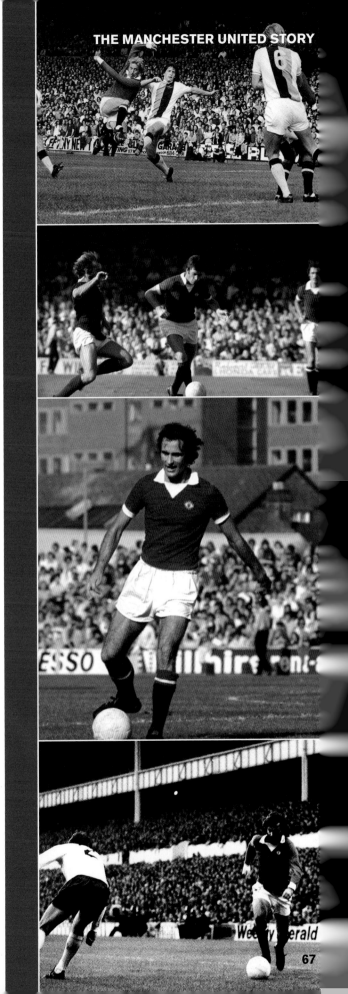

# 1974-75

Following the body blow of relegation, Tommy Docherty successfully rallied the troops ahead of the 1974-75 Second Division campaign to ensure Manchester United made an instant return to the top flight.

The Red Devils won the title by three points from Aston Villa, and stamped their authority on the division from the start, producing a nine-game unbeaten run at the start of the season to put themselves in pole position.

Two successive defeats in February were a body blow, but the team quickly regrouped and went 11 games without defeat to seal promotion, the season ending with a 4-0 win over Blackpool at Old Trafford in late April.

England striker Stuart Pearson top-scored with 17 league goals for the club, while Lou Macari chipped in with 11. But it was the United defence that was the real star of the season, proving the meanest in the division after conceding just 30 times in 42 games. The mainstays of Docherty's back line were goalkeeper Alex Stepney with 40 appearances, while centre-backs Martin Buchan and Brian Greenhoff played 41 and 39 games respectively. United were superb at Old Trafford, winning 17 of their 21 games and losing just once in front of their own fans, a 1-0 defeat to Bristol City in February.

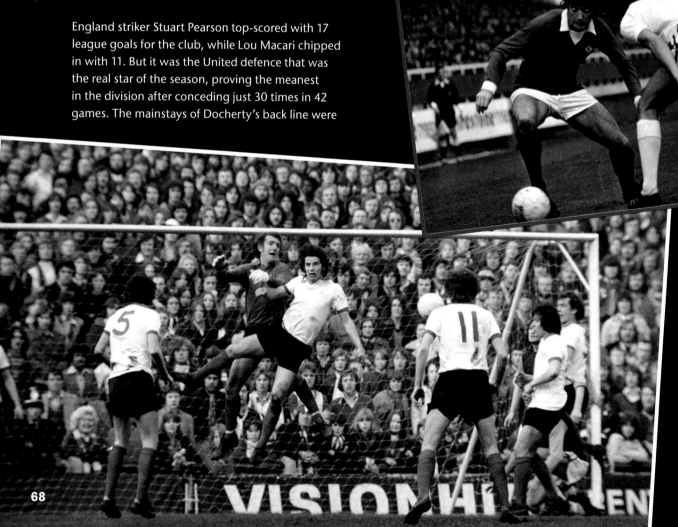

ENGLAND STRIKER STUART PEARSON TOP-SCORED WITH 17 LEAGUE GOALS FOR THE CLUB, WHILE LOU MACARI CHIPPED IN WITH 11

# FA CUP FINAL v LIVERPOOL

The 1977 FA Cup final saw Manchester United face Liverpool, and the game did not disappoint in terms of drama as the old rivals served up a hugely entertaining encounter at Wembley. The game was decided by a mad four-minute period in the second half, which produced all three of the game's goals.

Liverpool were the favourites, having clinched the First Division title earlier in the month, but it was United who drew first blood when Stuart Pearson opened the scoring in the 51st minute. The Merseysiders were level just two minutes later when Jimmy Case scored, but The Red Devils regained the lead in the 55th minute when Lou Macari's shot deflected off Jimmy Greenhoff and beat Ray Clemence in the Liverpool goal.

Despite Liverpool's desperate attempts for an equaliser, the United back four of Jimmy Nicholl, Brian Greenhoff, Martin Buchan and Arthur Albiston held firm for the remaining 35 minutes.

The Red Devils' 2-1 triumph was United's first success in the FA Cup in 14 years, and the only major silverware of Tommy Docherty's Old Trafford reign.

Just four days later Liverpool beat German champions Borussia Mönchengladbach in the final of the European Cup in Rome, but United's win in the FA Cup denied the Merseysiders a historic trophy treble, a feat United themselves would become the first English team to achieve in 1999.

FA Cup final 1977 Liverpool 1 v Manchester United 2. Nicholl, Greenhoff and Stepney celebrate with FA Cup. May, 1977

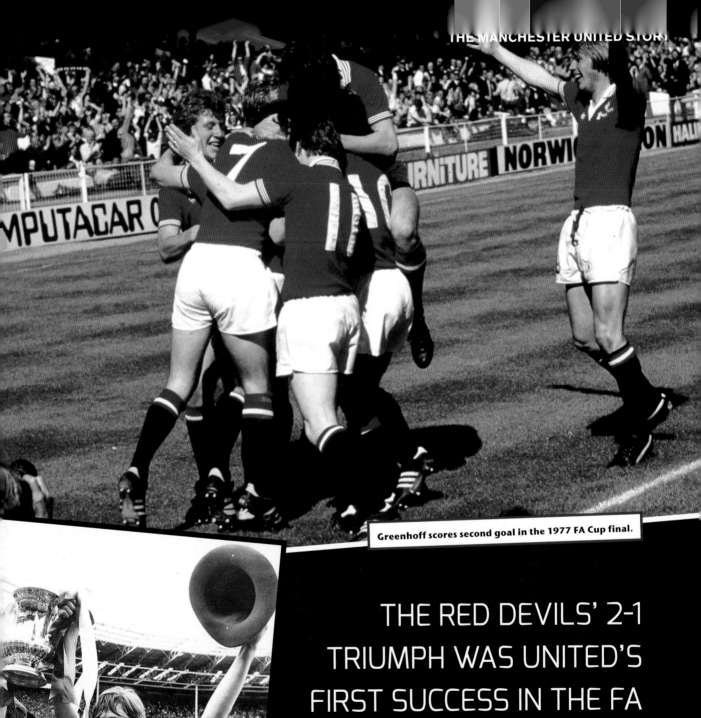

Greenhoff scores second goal in the 1977 FA Cup final.

THE RED DEVILS' 2-1 TRIUMPH WAS UNITED'S FIRST SUCCESS IN THE FA CUP IN 14 YEARS, AND THE ONLY MAJOR SILVERWARE OF TOMMY DOCHERTY'S

# 1977 FA CUP

A stalwart for Manchester United for more than a decade, Martin Buchan made over 450 appearances for the club and captained The Red Devils to their FA Cup win against Liverpool at Wembley in 1977.

The Scotland defender began his career with his hometown club Aberdeen, and was just 21 years old when he captained the Pittodrie side to a 3-1 victory against Celtic in the 1970 Scottish Cup final, becoming the youngest ever skipper to lift the trophy in the competition's history.

He headed south of the border two years later when Frank O'Farrell signed him in a £125,000 deal, at the time a club record fee, and made his debut for The Red Devils in March 1972 against Tottenham Hotspur at White Hart Lane.

The Scot captained the team for six of his 11 years at Old Trafford. As well as leading United to FA Cup glory, he skippered the side which shared the Charity Shield after a goalless draw with Liverpool in 1977. The stylish centre-half was also captain of the side that won the Second Division title in 1974-75 and promotion back to the top flight.

Buchan was also capped 34 times for his country and was part of the Scotland squad which played at the 1978 World Cup in Argentina. He left Old Trafford in 1983.

O'FARRELL SIGNED BUCHAN IN A £125,000 DEAL, AT THE TIME A CLUB RECORD FEE, AND BUCHAN MADE HIS DEBUT FOR THE RED DEVILS IN MARCH 1972

# 1977 CHARITY SHIELD v LIVERPOOL

Just two months after the sides had met at Wembley in the FA Cup final, Manchester United and Liverpool did it all again in the 1977 Charity Shield in front of a crowd of 82,000.

But while the first encounter had produced plenty of drama, the rematch produced little as the two clubs fought out a 0-0 draw and shared the Charity Shield.

United were now managed by Dave Sexton, who had replaced Tommy Docherty in the summer of 1977, but the new boss named exactly the same starting XI for the Charity Shield clash as the previous manager had done for the FA Cup final.

The game was a repeat of the 1965 Charity Shield clash between the two great rivals. That encounter had finished 2-2 at Old Trafford, but the defences were on top 12 years later. There was no extra-time, so after the 90 minutes the two clubs had to settle for a share of the trophy.

It was the eighth time United had claimed the trophy, and following the draw with Liverpool in 1965 and 3-3 scoreline against Tottenham Hotspur in 1967, the third time in a succession The Red Devils were joint winners. Sexton was United manager for nearly four years, but the Charity Shield would be the only trophy of his reign.

# 1980s

**1985 FA Cup final- Manchester United v Everton at Wembley Stadium.**
**Norman Whiteside celebrates with the trophy**

# THE 1980s

A modest decade in terms of the number of trophies won, the 1980s will forever be remembered in the history of Manchester United for the arrival of Alex Ferguson at Old Trafford and what would prove to be one of the most glittering managerial reigns the game has ever witnessed.

Before Ferguson, however, there was Ron Atkinson, who was named as Dave Sexton's successor in the summer of 1981 after a three-year stint at West Bromwich Albion in which he had forged his reputation by steering the unfashionable Baggies to two top-four finishes and the quarter-finals of the UEFA Cup.

Atkinson's Old Trafford tenure would last five full seasons. During his time with the club United never finished outside the top four in the First Division, but it was his side's outstanding performances in the FA Cup which grabbed the headlines as The Red Devils triumphed at Wembley twice in the space of two years.

The team's first success under Atkinson came in May 1983 when they beat Brighton & Hove Albion 4-0 in a replay, after the first game had ended deadlocked at 2-2. The Red Devils lifted the famous old trophy once again in 1985, when an iconic Norman Whiteside goal in extra-time at Wembley sealed a 1-0 victory over Everton. It was the sixth time United had won the FA Cup.

The 1986-87 season, however, was Atkinson's undoing as United began the campaign disappointingly, slipping to three successive defeats in the league. After a 4-1 defeat to Southampton in the League Cup in early November, the club decided he had taken the team as far as he could.

The search for a replacement was swift and for the fifth time in United's history, the club turned to a Scot to take charge of the first team when Alex Ferguson was unveiled as the new manager. It brought to an end his eight years at Aberdeen during which he had guided The Dons to three Scottish Premier Division titles, four Scottish FA Cups and the 1983 UEFA Cup Winners' Cup.

His CV was certainly impressive and although the United faithful would not witness the first of the deluge of trophies he amassed until the early 1990s, the remainder of the 1980s saw Ferguson steadily model the team in his own image and lay the foundations for the unprecedented glory years that lay ahead.

ATKINSON'S OLD TRAFFORD TENURE WOULD LAST FIVE FULL SEASONS. DURING HIS TIME WITH THE CLUB, UNITED NEVER FINISHED OUTSIDE THE TOP FOUR IN THE FIRST DIVISION

# FIRST DIVISION

|         | P  | W  | D  | L  | F  | A  | PTS | POS  |
|---------|----|----|----|----|----|----|-----|------|
| 1979-80 | 42 | 24 | 10 | 8  | 65 | 35 | 58  | 2nd  |
| 1980-81 | 42 | 15 | 18 | 9  | 51 | 36 | 48  | 8th  |
| 1981-82 | 42 | 22 | 12 | 8  | 59 | 29 | 78  | 3rd  |
| 1982-83 | 42 | 19 | 13 | 10 | 56 | 38 | 70  | 3rd  |
| 1983-84 | 42 | 20 | 14 | 8  | 71 | 41 | 74  | 4th  |
| 1984-85 | 42 | 22 | 10 | 10 | 77 | 47 | 76  | 4th  |
| 1985-86 | 42 | 22 | 10 | 10 | 70 | 36 | 76  | 4th  |
| 1986-87 | 42 | 14 | 14 | 14 | 52 | 45 | 56  | 11th |
| 1987-88 | 42 | 23 | 12 | 5  | 71 | 38 | 81  | 2nd  |
| 1988-89 | 38 | 13 | 12 | 13 | 45 | 35 | 51  | 11th |

# HONOURS

**FA Cup** 1983, 1985

**Charity Shield** 1983

# RON ATKINSON

## UNITED MANAGER 1981

Ron Atkinson had been in management for ten years when he was unveiled a Manchester United's new boss in the summer of 1981. And although he was unable to take The Red Devils back to the top of the First Division, his five yea at Old Trafford witnessed an upturn in the team's fortunes.

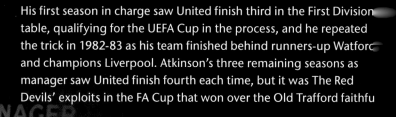

His first season in charge saw United finish third in the First Division table, qualifying for the UEFA Cup in the process, and he repeated the trick in 1982-83 as his team finished behind runners-up Watforc and champions Liverpool. Atkinson's three remaining seasons as manager saw United finish fourth each time, but it was The Red Devils' exploits in the FA Cup that won over the Old Trafford faithfu

His first success in the competition came in 1983. Although Brighton & Hove Albion held United to a 2-2 draw at Wembley in the final, Atkinson's team were on fire in the replay five days later as they hammered the Seagulls 4-0.

More FA Cup glory came in 1985. United saw off old rivals Liverpoo in a semi-final replay to set up a final with Everton, where an iconic Norman Whiteside goal at Wembley was the difference between the two sides.

The 1986-87 season, however, saw United win just one of their opening nine First Division fixtures, and despite his success in cup competitions, the club decided a new manager was needed and relieved Atkinson of his duties.

# ALEX FERGUSON

## UNITED MANAGER 1986

Alex Ferguson was 44 when he was named as Ron Atkinson's successor as Manchester United manager in November 1986. And although he had enjoyed a great deal of success in Scotland with St Mirren and then Aberdeen, he had never played or coached in England before.

Despite the fact it would take the Scot nearly four years to win his first trophy, his impact at Old Trafford was incredible. Under his leadership, United would be transformed from one of the biggest teams in England to without doubt one of the top sides in the world.

The early years of the Ferguson era saw him slowly transform the culture of the club and remodel the squad in his own image. Once United had lifted that first trophy, the 1990 FA Cup at Wembley, there was absolutely no stopping them.

The advent of the Premier League in 1992 saw The Red Devils crowned champions of England 13 times under the Scot, and before he finally brought his remarkable career to an end in 2013, United had also amassed five FA Cups, four League Cups, two Champions League crowns, the UEFA Cup Winners' Cup, the UEFA Super Cup, the Intercontinental Cup and the FIFA Club World Cup to make him the most successful manager in the history of the English game.

To the delight of the Old Trafford faithful, Ferguson's reign also saw United overtake Liverpool's previous record of 18 top flight crowns, with The Red Devils' 2012-13 Premier League title win taking the club's tally to 20.

"MY GREATEST CHALLENGE IS NOT WHAT'S HAPPENING AT THE MOMENT, MY GREATEST CHALLENGE WAS KNOCKING LIVERPOOL RIGHT OFF THEIR PERCH. AND YOU CAN PRINT THAT."

ALEX FERGUSON

# TROPHIES WON
## UNDER ALEX FERGUSON

### PREMIER LEAGUE

| | | | | |
|---|---|---|---|---|
| 1993 | 1994 | 1996 | 1997 | 1999 |
| 2000 | 2001 | 2003 | 2007 | 2008 |
| 2009 | 2011 | 2013 | | |

### FA CUP

| | | | | |
|---|---|---|---|---|
| 1990 | 1994 | 1996 | 1999 | 2004 |

### COMMUNITY SHIELD

| | | | | |
|---|---|---|---|---|
| 1990 | 1993 | 1994 | 1996 | 1997 |
| 2003 | 2007 | 2008 | 2010 | 2011 |

### LEAGUE CUP

| | | | |
|---|---|---|---|
| 1992 | 2006 | 2009 | 2010 |

### CHAMPIONS LEAGUE

| | |
|---|---|
| 1999 | 2008 |

### FIFA CLUB WORLD CUP

2008

### UEFA SUPER CUP

1991

### UEFA CUP WINNERS' CUP

1991

ANDERSON ou
ESTABLISHED
HIMSELF IN THE
FIRST TEAM
HIS FIRST SEASON
HE MADE 50
APPEARANCES IN
ALL COMPETITIONS

# VIV ANDERSON

Alex Ferguson's incredible 27 years as Manchester United manager saw the club sign well over 100 players, but his first came in 1987 when he signed full-back Viv Anderson for £250,000 from Arsenal.

At 31, Anderson was in the autumn of his career, but Ferguson was convinced his experience was vital. Anderson quickly established himself in the first team and in his first season he made 38 appearances in all competitions, starting 30 of The Red Devils' 40 First Division games as the team finished runners-up.

He never won a trophy at Old Trafford, but his arrival under Ferguson signalled a change of direction for United. Anderson left the club in 1991 when he joined Sheffield Wednesday, and he finally ended his playing days in 1995 after making two league appearances for Middlesbrough.

At international level, Anderson made history when he made his debut for England in November 1978 against Czechoslovakia, in the process becoming the first black player to represent the Three Lions.

He went on to win 30 caps in total for his country, scoring twice, and was part of the England squad for the 1982 World Cup in Spain, and again for the finals in Mexico four years later.

# 1990s

Manchester United v Crystal Palace - FA Cup final Replay — May, 1990

# THE 1990s

If the 1980s was the decade in which Alex Ferguson laid his foundations at Old Trafford, the 1990s was the period in which Manchester United reaped the rewards as The Red Devils enjoyed unprecedented domestic and European success.

It started in May 1990, when Ferguson's side overcame Crystal Palace at Wembley in the FA Cup final replay. The win was the beginning of an incredible period of success and in every season throughout the decade, United would lift at least one trophy.

In 1991, The Red Devils made their mark in Europe by beating Barcelona in the final of the Cup Winners' Cup and Red Star Belgrade in the UEFA Super Cup. In 1992, they beat Nottingham Forest to win the League Cup, but it was league glory that the Old Trafford faithful wanted after 26 long years.

United had not been crowned champions since 1967, but the wait for the title finally came to an end in 1992-93, the first season of the Premier League. Ferguson's side swept all before them to finish top of the table, ten points clear of second-placed Aston Villa. The team was beaten only six times in the league that season.

The Red Devils would win the Premier League another four times by the end of the decade, twice successfully defending the title. They also lifted the FA Cup three more times following their 1990 success and five Charity Shields, and their dominance of the English game was without doubt.

Ferguson, however, wasn't content with just domestic honours, and the 1990s ended with two of the club's most memorable victories on foreign soil.

The first came in May 1999 at the Nou Camp, when The Red Devils faced German giants Bayern Munich in the final of the Champions League with. United losing 1-0 as the game entered injury-time, dramatic strikes from Teddy Sheringham and Ole Gunnar Solskjaer secured an incredible 2-1 win. It was a result that also secured United's unprecedented trophy treble after winning the Premier League and FA Cup.

Six months later, Ferguson's team travelled to Japan to play in the Intercontinental Cup. South American champions Palmeiras were the opponents in Tokyo, but the Brazilians were unable to stop United, with a first-half goal from skipper Roy Keane enough to see The Red Devils claim the title of the best club side on the planet.

FERGUSON, HOWEVER, WASN'T CONTENT WITH JUST DOMESTIC HONOURS, AND THE 1990s ENDED WITH TWO OF THE CLUB'S MOST MEMORABLE VICTORIES ON FOREIGN SOIL

# FIRST DIVISION

| | P | W | D | L | F | A | PTS | POS |
|---|---|---|---|---|---|---|---|---|
| 1989-90 | 38 | 13 | 9 | 16 | 46 | 47 | 48 | 13th |
| 1990-91 | 38 | 16 | 12 | 10 | 58 | 45 | 59 | 6th |
| 1991-92 | 42 | 21 | 15 | 6 | 63 | 33 | 78 | 2nd |

# PREMIER LEAGUE

| | P | W | D | L | F | A | PTS | POS |
|---|---|---|---|---|---|---|---|---|
| 1992-93 | 42 | 24 | 12 | 6 | 67 | 31 | 84 | 1st |
| 1993-94 | 42 | 27 | 11 | 4 | 80 | 38 | 92 | 1st |
| 1994-95 | 42 | 26 | 10 | 6 | 77 | 28 | 88 | 2nd |
| 1995-96 | 38 | 25 | 7 | 6 | 73 | 35 | 82 | 1st |
| 1996-97 | 38 | 21 | 12 | 5 | 76 | 44 | 75 | 1st |
| 1997-98 | 38 | 23 | 8 | 7 | 73 | 26 | 77 | 2nd |
| 1998-99 | 38 | 22 | 13 | 3 | 80 | 37 | 79 | 1st |

# HONOURS

**Premier League** 192-93, 1993-94, 1995-96, 1996-97, 1998-99

**FA Cup** 1990, 1994, 1996, 1999

**League Cup** 1992

**Charity Shield** 1990, 1993, 1994, 1996, 1997

**Champions League** 1999

**UEFA Cup Winners' Cup** 1991

**UEFA Super Cup** 1991

**Intercontinental Cup** 1999

# 1990 FA CUP FINAL V CRYSTAL PALACE

After three-and-a-half years in the Manchester United hot-seat without a trophy, the pressure was growing on Alex Ferguson to deliver. But he did just that in May 1990 as The Red Devils eventually overcame a stubborn Crystal Palace side in the final of the FA Cup.

Some 80,000 supporters watched the games at Wembley in a thrilling games that finished 2-2 after 90 minutes, thanks to goals from captain Bryan Robson and striker Mark Hughes. The Eagles took then took a 3-2 lead two minutes into extra-time, but The Red Devils were rescued seven minutes from time with Hughes' second goal of the game to ensure the final went to a replay.

They returned five days later, but the rematch proved to be a much tighter affair in front of another sell-out crowd. The clash was settled in the 55th minute when full-back Lee Martin latched on to a pass from midfielder Neil Webb and fired the ball past Nigel Martyn in the Crystal Palace goal.

United held firm in the face of an Eagles fightback, and when the final whistle sounded, Robson climbed the famous Wembley steps to lift the FA Cup for the third time in his career.

Ferguson had silenced his critics and, buoyed by their first trophy with him in charge, United would go from strength to strength.

# ROBSON CLIMBED THE FAMOUS WEMBLEY STEPS TO LIFT THE FA CUP FOR THE THIRD TIME IN HIS CAREER

# 1992 LEAGUE CUP FINAL

**The League Cup had not brought much success to Manchester United until 1992, when they reached the final of the competition for only the third time in the club's history.**

The Red Devils' two previous attempts to lift the trophy had ended in a 2-1 loss to Liverpool in 1983 and a 1-0 defeat against Sheffield Wednesday in 1991. But it was third time lucky 12 months later, as Alex Ferguson's side saw off the challenge of Nottingham Forest at Wembley.

United had beaten Cambridge United, Portsmouth, Oldham Athletic, Leeds United and Middlesbrough on their way to the final, but found Forest tough opposition. The Red Devils had lost 1-0 to Brian

Clough's side in the league the previous month, but the roles were reversed as they struck in 14th minute with a goal from Brian McClair. The Scotland midfielder took a pass from Ryan Giggs before dribbling into the area and hitting a low drive past the Forest goalkeeper Andy Marrriott into the right hand corner.

It proved to be the only goal of the game and when the final whistle sounded, Ferguson had secured the second trophy of his Old Trafford career.

UNITED HAD BEATEN
CAMBRIDGE UNITED,
PORTSMOUTH,
OLDHAM ATHLETIC,
LEEDS UNITED AND
MIDDLESBROUGH
ON THEIR WAY TO
THE FINAL

# 1992-93 PREMIER LEAGUE TROPHY

With an FA Cup and League Cup on his CV, Alex Ferguson made no secret of his desire to add a league title to the list. And his team gave it to their manager in 1992-93, when they triumphed in the first Premier League campaign.

| | P | W | D | L | F | A | PTS | POS |
|---|---|---|---|---|---|---|---|---|
| 1992-93 | 42 | 24 | 12 | 6 | 67 | 31 | 84 | 1st |

The season couldn't have got off to a worse start, as the team suffered back-to-back defeats against Sheffield United and Everton, but the initial setbacks only stiffened the side's resolve and over the next 40 matches, The Red Devils would be beaten only four more times.

In fact, United finished the season with seven wins on the spin, including a 3-0 win against Chelsea at Old Trafford in April which sealed the title by ten points from runners-up Aston Villa. It was the club's first success since Matt Busby had masterminded United's title win in 1967.

Old Trafford legend Mark Hughes led the way in front of goal, top-scoring for the team with 15 goals in the Premier League, while Ryan Giggs, Eric Cantona and Brian McClair each found the back of the net nine times.

In terms of starting appearances, there were just two ever presents in the team's 42 Premier League fixtures. They were Danish goalkeeper Peter Schmeichel, in his second season with the club, and England centre-back Gary Pallister while McClair started 41 times in the league and came off the bench once.

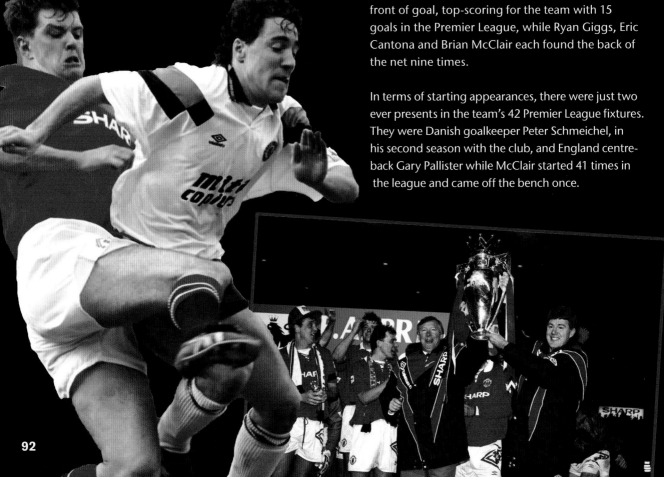

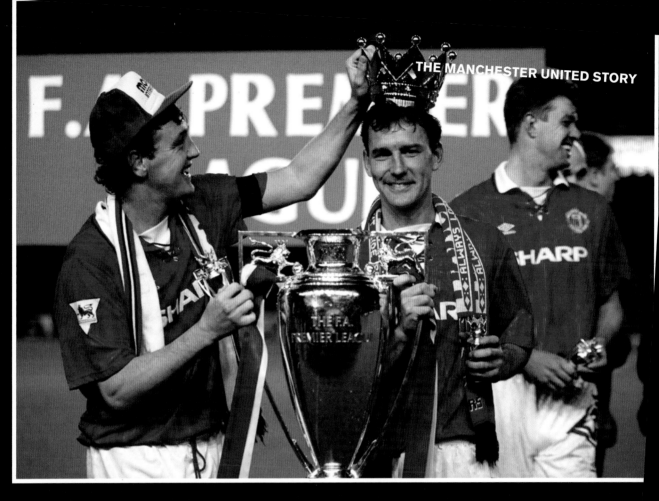

OLD TRAFFORD LEGEND MARK HUGHES LED THE WAY
IN FRONT OF GOAL, TOP-SCORING FOR THE TEAM
WITH 15 GOALS IN THE PREMIER LEAGUE

# ERIC CANTONA

Signed from Leeds United in November 1992 in a £1.2million deal, Eric Cantona spent only five years at Old Trafford but made a huge impact on the club, helping The Red Devils lift six major trophies.

The French forward enjoyed his most prolific season in 1993-94, top-scoring for The Red Devils with 25 goals from 49 games in all competitions. Cantona found the back of the net 18 times in the Premier League as United successfully defended their title, and also hit four goals in five games in the FA Cup.

Two of those four came from the penalty spot in the final at Wembley against Chelsea. United beat the Blues 4-0 to lift the trophy for the eighth time, and claim a league and cup double for the first time in the club's history.

Cantona's superb form during the season saw him named the Professional Footballers Association Player of the Year for 1992-93, becoming only the third United star to collect the award after Mark Hughes and Gary Pallister.

The Frenchman left Old Trafford in 1997 at the age of 31, when he retired from the game. He had scored 82 goals in 185 appearances for The Red Devils and won four Premier League titles and two FA Cups with the club.

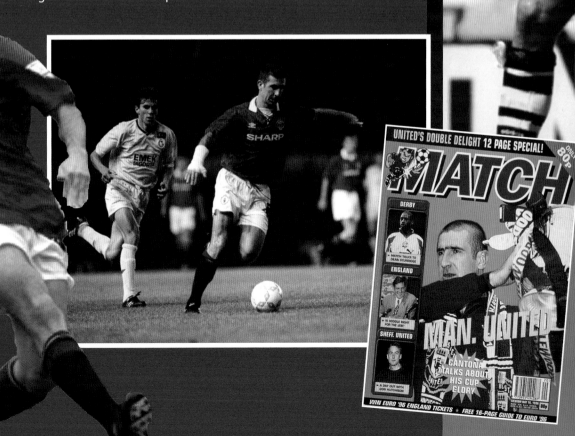

"IF EVER THERE WAS ONE PLAYER, ANYWHERE IN THE WORLD, THAT WAS MADE FOR MANCHESTER UNITED, IT WAS CANTONA. HE SWAGGERED IN, STUCK HIS CHEST OUT, RAISED HIS HEAD AND SURVEYED EVERYTHING AS THOUGH HE WERE ASKING: 'I'M CANTONA. HOW BIG ARE YOU? ARE YOU BIG ENOUGH FOR ME?''

ALEX FERGUSON

# 1994 **FA CUP FINAL** v **CHELSEA**

The 1994 FA Cup final between Manchester United and Chelsea at Wembley was the most one-sided final that decade, as Alex Ferguson's team brushed aside Glenn Hoddle's Blues convincingly to lift the trophy.

United had enjoyed a fairly easy passage to the final, scoring 14 goals and conceding just three, and the final caused few problems as the rampant Red Devils put Chelsea to the sword.

Captained by centre-back Steve Bruce, United were unable to unlock The Blues defence in the opening 45 minutes but took the lead on the hour mark when Eric Cantona was on target from the penalty

spot. Six minutes later, the advantage was doubled when the French striker once again beat Chelsea keeper Dmitri Kharine from the spot.

The Red Devils were now firmly in control and further goals from Mark Hughes, in the 69th minute, and Brian McClair's injury-time strike, rubbed the salt into Chelsea wounds.

The Red Devils' 4-0 battering saw United claim the league and FA Cup double for the first time in their history. In doing so, they became only the sixth club in England to achieve the feat, after Preston North End and Aston Villa in the 19th century and Tottenham Hotspur, Arsenal and Liverpool in the 20th century.

"I WENT OVER TO TAKE A KICK WHERE THE CHELSEA FANS WERE AND THEY STARTED CHUCKING STICKS OF CELERY AND SWEETCORN. IT MADE ME LAUGH TO THINK OF THEM POPPING INTO GREENGROCERS' SHOPS ON THE WAY TO WEMBLEY."

RYAN GIGGS AFTER THE FA CUP FINAL
MANCHESTER UNITED v CHELSEA, 1994

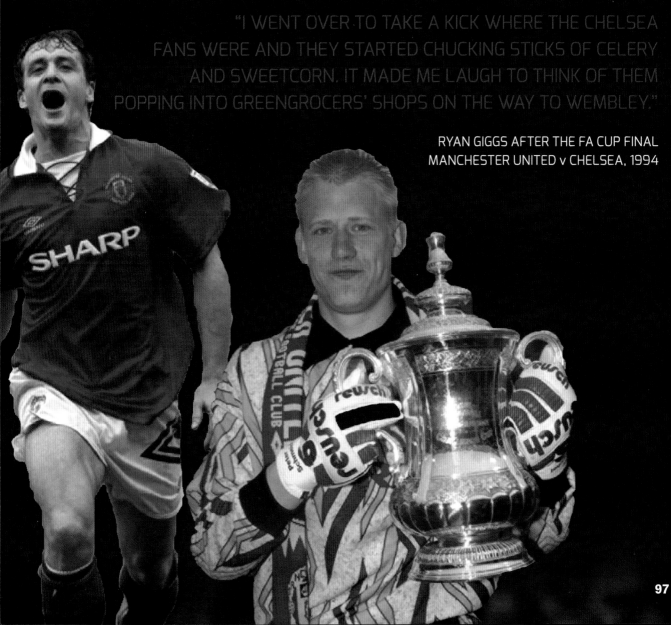

# 1995-96 SEASON

Manchester United lost their Premier League crown to Blackburn Rovers in 1994-95, but Alex Ferguson's boys reclaimed it in style the following season after an epic battle with Newcastle United.

Although The Red Devils were briefly top of the table in September after a 3-0 win over Bolton Wanderers, they spent most of the season chasing the free-scoring Magpies and it wasn't until late March that United overtook their title rivals and put themselves back in pole position.

The start of the United revival was Eric Cantona, who scored in six successive Premier League games in March and April to spearhead the fightback. Seven wins from their final eight league games, including a 3-2 victory over Manchester City at Maine Road, was enough to break the Newcastle challenge. Cantona's 14 goals that season made him United's top scorer in the Premier League, while the only other Red Devil to reach double figures was midfielder Paul Scholes with ten.

It was a season in which Ferguson made full use of his squad, and a total of 23 players played for United during their Premier League campaign. Striker Andy Cole was the busiest of the outfield players with 32 starts and two substitute appearances, while Ryan Giggs and David Beckham both played 33 times each.

United went on to beat Liverpool 1-0 in the 1996 FA Cup final at Wembley, completing the league and cup double for the second time in two years.

UNITED WENT ON TO BEAT
LIVERPOOL 1-0 IN THE 1996 FA CUP
FINAL AT WEMBLEY, COMPLETING
THE LEAGUE AND CUP DOUBLE FOR
THE SECOND TIME IN TWO YEARS

1

2

3

4

# ALL TIME
# MANCHESTER UNITED
# TOP GOALSCORERS

1. Sir Bobby Charlton – 249
2. Denis Law – 237
3. Wayne Rooney – 237
4. Jack Rowley – 211
5. George Best – 179
6. Dennis Viollet – 179
7. Ryan Giggs – 168
8. Joe Spence – 168
9. Mark Hughes – 163
10. Paul Scholes – 155

7

5

6

8

9

10

# 1996-97 SEASON

If the battle between Manchester United and Newcastle for the title in 1995-96 proved an epic and entertaining tussle, the fight between the clubs for honours the following season was far more straightforward.

The final table again saw United finish on top with the Magpies in second, but the gap of seven points between the two clubs compared to the four the previous season told its own story, and in truth Alex Ferguson's team were never in danger of giving up their crown.

United made an unconvincing start to the campaign, with just one victory in their opening four games. But they soon found their form and, buoyed by a 1-0 win over Liverpool at Old Trafford in October, they began to climb the table.

The key moment that season, however, came in early February, when the team beat Southampton 2-1. It was a result that sent The Red Devils to the top of the table, and it was a position they would not give up for the rest of the season.

United were the division's top scorers with 76 goals from 38 games, with Ole Gunnar Solskjaer finishing as top scorer with 18 goals from 33 appearances. Eric Cantona also reached double figures with 11, while another 12 players got their name on the scoresheet for The Red Devils in the Premier League.

THE KEY MOMENT THAT SEASON, HOWEVER, CAME IN EARLY FEBRUARY, WHEN THE TEAM BEAT SOUTHAMPTON 2-1

"WITH ANDY COLE UP FRONT
THEY CAN SCORE AT ANY TIME."
LAURENT ROBERT

# ANDY COLE

Although he had already scored 32 goals in just 88 appearances in his first three seasons at Old Trafford, it was during the 1997-98 campaign that Andy Cole really established himself at Manchester United.

Signed from Newcastle United in January 1995 for a then record British transfer fee of £7million, the England striker began the season quietly. But once he had opened his account in a 3-0 victory over Coventry in late August, there was no stopping him and he finished as the club's top scorer with 25 goals in all competitions.

He scored 15 in the Premier League, netting the only hat-trick of United's season in a 7-0 drubbing of Barnsley at Old Trafford in October, while his brace in early December was key in The Red Devils' 3-1 victory over Liverpool at Anfield.

The striker scored five in just four appearances in the FA Cup and was also on target against Slovakian side FC Kosice and Dutch team Feyenoord in the group stages of the Champions League.

Cole spent three more years at Old Trafford before signing for Blackburn Rovers in the summer of 2001. He left The Red Devils having scored 121 goals for the club in 275 games, a record that leaves him 17th on the list of United's top scorers and one place ahead of Cristiano Ronaldo.

Cole was capped 15 times by England between 1995 and 2002 but struggled to transform his form onto the international stage, scoring just once for the Three Lions.

# ALEX FERGUSON

Manchester United enjoyed many great seasons under Alex Ferguson, but none were better than the 1998-99 campaign. The Red Devils rewrote the record books and became the first, and still only, club in the history of English football to complete the League, FA Cup and European Cup treble.

An amazing run of 33 games unbeaten in all competitions, which began on Boxing Day with a 3-0 win over Nottingham Forest, was the catalyst for The Red Devils' incredible achievement. By the end of the season, United had clinched all three trophies in the space of ten days.

The Premier League title was won on May 16, the last day of the season, when Ferguson's side recovered from going a goal behind to Tottenham Hotspur at Old Trafford to win 2-1. David Beckham and Andy Cole scored the goals that saw United take the title ahead of Arsenal by a single point.

Just six days later, United returned to London to face Newcastle United in the FA Cup final at Wembley and the second leg of the treble was clinched. The Red Devils won 2-0, with the goals coming from Teddy Sheringham and Paul Scholes either side of half-time.

The team had only four days rest ahead of their Champions League final against Bayern Munich in Barcelona. But United's staying power was phenomenal, with Sheringham and Ole Gunnar Solskjaer both scoring in injury-time to grab a 2-1 win and earn The Red Devils a place in football folklore.

The 1999 FA Cup was the 15th time Manchester United had reached the final, and they claimed their tenth win after a 2-0 victory over Newcastle United.

A crowd of over 79,000 was at Wembley for the match, and they didn't have to wait long for the newly-crowned Premier League champions to take charge, scoring as early as the 11th minute.

Striker Teddy Sheringham had only been on the pitch for two minutes after replacing injured skipper Roy Keane, but the England international was alert enough to collect Paul Scholes' pass and hit a low drive past Magpies goalkeeper Steve Harper.

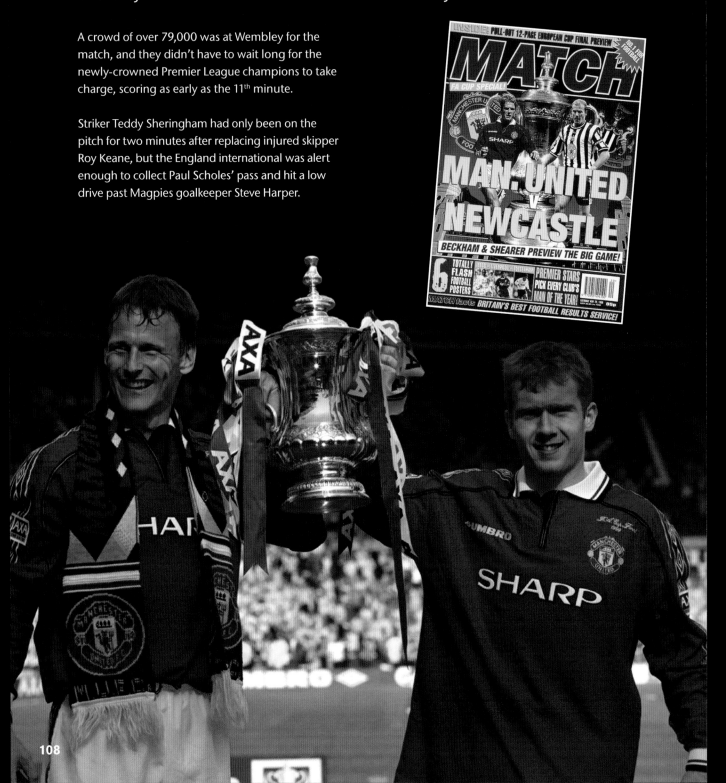

It was 1-0 to United at the break, but just as they had done in the first half, The Red Devils struck early after the restart. Sheringham repaid the favour to Scholes, rolling the ball into the midfielder's path, and the midfielder made no mistake with his 20-yard strike.

Newcastle didn't have a reply and when the whistle went for full time, the FA Cup was on its way to Old Trafford for the fourth time in the 1990s.

More significantly, the victory meant United remained on course for a historic treble, and the chance to become the first English side to win the League, FA and European Cups in the same season.

# 1999 CHAMPIONS LEAGUE

In one of the most dramatic games in European Cup history, Manchester United scored two injury-time goals to win the 1999 Champions League and claim an incredible treble.

Alex Ferguson's side had gone behind against Bayern Munich in the sixth minute of the match, when winger Mario Basler scored with a free-kick. Despite having more possession and attempts on goal in the remainder of the contest, it seemed United's dreams of winning the trophy were over.

The final went into three minutes of second-half injury-time with Bayern still leading 1-0, but 36 seconds into it United handed themselves a lifeline when Teddy Sheringham instinctively redirected a wayward shot into the back of the net for the equaliser.

Two minutes and 17 seconds of the added time had passed when Ferguson's side struck again, Ole Gunnar Solskjaer reacting quickest to Sheringham's glancing header to stab the ball past Oliver Khan and into the roof of the Bayern goal. There was no time for the Germans to respond, and for a second time United were the champions of Europe.

Their triumph in Spain also sealed the Treble and ensured the team of 1998-99 would be remembered forever as one which made football history.

THERE WAS NO TIME FOR THE GERMANS TO RESPOND, AND FOR A SECOND TIME UNITED WERE THE CHAMPIONS OF EUROPE

# 2000s

**Manchester United v Juventus. July 2003**

# THE 2000s

The 2000s saw the dawn of a new Millennium, but it was very much business as usual at Old Trafford as The Red Devils continued to dominate English football, adding six more Premier League crowns and a third Champions League success to the club's collection.

There were also three League Cup triumphs and victory in the 2008 FIFA Club World Cup to celebrate, as United underlined their status as one of the world's most successful clubs.

In terms of the league, the highlight was the side's incredible achievement of claiming three consecutive titles on two separate occasions. Alex Ferguson's team first completed the feat in 2000-01, when they finished ten points clear of Arsenal to secure a Premier League treble, and they repeated the trick in 2008-09 when they beat Liverpool to become champions for a third successive season.

They were also champions in 2002-03, the club's 15th league success, when 25 goals from Ruud van Nistelrooy ensured The Red Devils finished the campaign in top spot ahead of Arsenal.

Europe was still high on United's agenda, and nine years after their famous last-gasp Champions League victory over Bayern Munich, The Red Devils won it again after beating Chelsea on penalties in Moscow in 2008.

United also did well in domestic cup competitions, and having won the League Cup just once previously, United claimed the trophy three times in the space of four years. Ferguson's men beat Wigan 4-0 in 2006 to start the run, before overcoming Tottenham Hotspur on penalties in 2009 and then successfully defending their trophy in 2010 with a 2-1 victory over Aston Villa.

There was also an 11th FA Cup triumph for the United faithful to enjoy, as a brace from Van Nistelrooy and a one from Cristiano Ronaldo wrapped up a 3-0 win over Millwall at the Millennium Stadium.

It was a successful decade by anyone's standards, but United weren't finished. After lifting domestic and European trophies, The Red Devils made their mark on the global game when they headed to Japan to compete in the 2008 FIFA Club World Cup. United beat Liga de Quito from Ecuador 1-0 in the final to be officially crowned the best club team on the planet.

THERE WAS ALSO AN 11TH FA CUP TRIUMPH FOR THE UNITED FAITHFUL TO ENJOY, AS A BRACE FROM VAN NISTELROOY AND ONE FROM CRISTIANO RONALDO WRAPPED UP A 3-0 WIN OVER MILLWALL AT THE MILLENNIUM STADIUM

# PREMIER LEAGUE

|         | P  | W  | D  | L | F  | A  | PTS | POS |
|---------|----|----|----|---|----|----|-----|-----|
| 1999-00 | 38 | 28 | 7  | 3 | 97 | 45 | 91  | 1st |
| 2000-01 | 38 | 24 | 8  | 6 | 79 | 31 | 80  | 1st |
| 2001-02 | 38 | 24 | 5  | 9 | 87 | 45 | 77  | 3rd |
| 2002-03 | 38 | 25 | 8  | 5 | 74 | 34 | 83  | 1st |
| 2003-04 | 38 | 23 | 6  | 9 | 64 | 35 | 75  | 3rd |
| 2004-05 | 38 | 22 | 11 | 5 | 58 | 26 | 77  | 3rd |
| 2005-06 | 38 | 25 | 8  | 5 | 72 | 34 | 83  | 2nd |
| 2006-07 | 38 | 28 | 5  | 5 | 83 | 27 | 89  | 1st |
| 2007-08 | 38 | 27 | 6  | 5 | 80 | 22 | 87  | 1st |
| 2008-09 | 38 | 28 | 6  | 4 | 68 | 24 | 90  | 1st |

# HONOURS

**Premier League** 1999-00, 2000-01, 2002-03, 2006-07, 2007-08, 2008-09

**FA Cup** 2004

**League Cup** 2006, 2009

**Community Shield** 2003, 2007, 2008

**Champions League** 2008

**FIFA Club World Cup** 2008

# 1999-2000

The start of the 2000s saw United, defending Premier League champions, sitting second in the table. But a 1-0 victory over Middlesbrough at the end of month, courtesy of a David Beckham strike, saw The Red Devils move into top spot – and that's where they stayed for the rest of the season.

The win over 'Boro brought an end to United's patchy form over Christmas and New Year, and in their remaining 17 league games, Alex Ferguson's team suffered just one defeat.

The Red Devils tore apart West Ham United 7-1, and picked up 4-0 victories against Bradford and Sunderland. Their dominance in the second half of the season meant that after 38 games, United were an incredible 18 points ahead of the Gunners, which is still the biggest winning margin in Premier League history.

The team scored an incredible 97 goals during the campaign, and only two sides – Chelsea and Newcastle United – were able to keep a clean sheet against United's deadly attack. They were beaten only three times in 38 fixtures, but all of those came away from home and no team came away from Old Trafford in 1999-2000 with three points.

No player was an ever-present for The Red Devils during the season, but striker Dwight Yorke made the most appearances with 32, closely followed by David Beckham, Mikael Silvestre and Paul Scholes with 31 each.

# DWIGHT YORKE

gned from Premier League rivals Aston Villa in the summer of 1998 for
12.6million, Dwight Yorke was a key member of the treble-winning side of
999. But the Trinidad & Tobago striker's contribution in 1999-2000 was just
s important as United successfully defended their Premier League title.

orke began the season with United's only goal in a
-1 draw with Everton at Goodison Park in August,
and he was on target in four of the club's opening
ive league fixtures as Alex Ferguson's side went top
of the table.

His run continued throughout the year, and he hit a
hat-trick in March when Derby County were beaten
3-1 at Old Trafford. The following month he netted
a brace in a 3-2 win over Chelsea, although by now
United had already been confirmed as the runaway
champions. Yorke top-scored for United in the
league with 20 goals, and 24 in all competitions,
and in March he was named the Premier League
Player of the Month.

Yorke enjoyed two more seasons at Old Trafford
before he left the club in the summer of 2002 to
join Blackburn Rovers. In just four years as a Red
Devil, the striker won three Premier League titles,
the FA Cup and, the Champions League and the
1999 Intercontinental Cup.

He scored 66 goals in 152 appearances in
total, which makes him 33rd on the United's
all-time list and just one goal behind the great
Norman Whiteside.

# 2000-01 LEAGUE

The 2000-01 season was a historic one as United became the first and only club to complete a hat-trick of Premier League titles, The Red Devils claiming their third successive league crown with ten points to spare.

Three other clubs – Huddersfield Town in the 1920s, Arsenal the following decade and Liverpool in the 80s – had won the old First Division three years on the trot, but until United's success in 2001, no team had been able to repeat their achievement in the Premier League era.

Alex Ferguson's side did so in style. A 3-0 victory over Leicester City at Filbert Street in mid-October took the team to the top of the table and for the remaining seven months of the campaign, United remained

THEIR LEAD WAS SO BIG THAT THEY WERE ABLE TO LOSE THEIR FINAL THREE LEAGUE GAMES OF THE SEASON AND STILL FINISH HANDSOMELY AHEAD OF RUNNERS-UP ARSENAL

untroubled in first place in the Premier League. Their lead was so big that they were able to lose their final three league games of the season and still finish handsomely ahead of runners-up Arsenal.

England striker Teddy Sheringham led the way for United up front, top-scoring with 15 league goals, but there were also impressive contributions from Ole Gunnar Solskjaer with ten, while David Beckham, Dwight Yorke and Andy Cole all chipped in with nine.

Not for the first time, the club's homegrown talent was the mainstay of the title-winning side. Midfielder Paul Scholes made the most appearances in the Premier League with 32 games under his belt, while Ryan Giggs and Beckham were just behind with 31 matches each.

# 2002-03
# PREMIER LEAGUE

After securing three successive Premier League titles, Manchester United's standards slipped in 2001-02 as they surrendered the silverware to Arsenal, but Alex Ferguson's side roared back to the summit of the English game the following season to reclaim their crown.

An unconvincing start to the campaign saw The Red Devils slip down to 10th in the table in September after back-to-back defeats to Bolton Wanderers and Leeds United. Although results improved after that, the side's 3-1 defeat away to Middlesbrough on Boxing Day saw United still off the pace in third.

It was time for the team to stand up and be counted and the players did so in style, stringing together an 18-match unbeaten run, including seven clean sheets, which took them above Newcastle United and then Arsenal to the title once again.

The highlight of the run was the 4-0 demolition of Liverpool at Old Trafford in early April, while just 11 days later the team travelled to London to face Arsenal at Highbury and made sure The Gunners would not be in a position to make a late charge by grabbing a crucial 2-2 draw.

Arsenal outscored United in the league with 85 goals to 74, but it was The Red Devils' back four that secured the silverware, conceding just 34 times in 38 fixtures.

## IT WAS THE RED DEVILS' BACK FOUR WHO SECURED THE SILVERWARE, CONCEDING JUST 34 TIMES IN 38 FIXTURES

# FA CUP FINAL

There was no 16th league title for Manchester United in 2003-04, but any disappointment the Old Trafford faithful felt was eased a little with an FA Cup final triumph.

United's route to the final was eventful, drawing Aston Villa in the third round before overcoming neighbours Manchester City in a 4-2 thriller in the fifth round and beating Arsenal 1-0 in the semi-finals at Villa Park courtesy of a Paul Scholes goal.

Their opponents in the final were First Division Millwall, but any hopes the London side had of pulling off a shock were extinguished by a ruthless display by The Red Devils at the Millennium Stadium.

# WHEN CRISTIANO RONALDO STOLE IN AHEAD OF THE LIONS' DEFENCE TO HEAD HOME GARY NEVILLE'S CROSS, THE WRITING WAS ON THE WALL

Millwall kept United at bay until the 44th minute, but when Cristiano Ronaldo stole in ahead of The Lions' defence to head home Gary Neville's cross, the writing was on the wall.

The second half belonged to Ruud van Nistelrooy. The Dutchman opened his account in the 65th minute when Ryan Giggs was brought down in the box and the striker scored from the penalty spot. He made it 3-0 to United nine minutes from the end when he made no mistake from three yards out following a Giggs pass, taking The Red Devils to a record 11th FA Cup win.

# SEASON

No-one has made more Manchester United appearances than the 963 made by Ryan Giggs, and the mercurial Welsh winger clocked up 44 matches in 2006-07 as The Red Devils were crowned Premier League champions again.

A total of 30 of those 44 appearances came in the league, as Alex Ferguson's side saw off the challenge of defending champions Chelsea, beating Jose Mourinho's team to the title by a six-point margin to give Giggs the ninth of his 13 Premier League triumphs.

The evergreen Welshman was 32 at the start of the season, but it proved to be another vintage campaign for him. Winning strikes in successive matches against Watford in August and Tottenham in September proved he had not lost his eye for goal.

Giggs was also in outstanding form in Europe, scoring in the Champions League group stage against Benfica at Old Trafford and then finding the back of the net in the last 16 clash with Lille in France.

The most decorated player in Manchester United's history, Giggs finally hung up his boots at the end of the 2013-14 season. He scored 168 times in his 963 appearances for the club, a total only bettered by six players, but his value to the team was so much more than just goals.

"WHEN HE'S AT THE TOP OF HIS GAME, THERE'S NOT A TEAM IN THE WORLD THAT CAN HANDLE GIGGS' SPEED AND PENETRATION"

SIR ALEX FERGUSON

# 2007-08
# SEASON

Cristiano Ronaldo spent six explosive seasons with The Red Devils, and enjoyed his most prolific campaign for the club in 2007-08 as Manchester United claimed a famous Premier League and Champions League double.

It was to be the Portuguese ace's penultimate season in England before signing for Real Madrid, and Ronaldo made it count with a phenomenal 42 goals in just 49 appearances for Alex Ferguson's all-conquering side.

The star was in particularly devastating form in the Premier League, with 31 goals in 34 matches. It was enough to earn him the Golden Boot award, as United finished two points clear of Chelsea to secure the club's 17th top-flight title. Ronaldo scored a hat-trick in January in a 6-0 thrashing of Newcastle United, while in March and April, he scored in six successive league games, including strikes in victories over Liverpool and Arsenal at Old Trafford.

He was just as deadly in Europe, with eight goals in 11 games, and it was his powerful header that opened the scoring in the Champions League final against Chelsea, a match which United won dramatically on penalties.

Unsurprisingly, his superb displays saw Ronaldo collect a series of individual awards. By the end of 2008 he had won the Ballon d'Or and been voted the FIFA World Player of the Year, as well as being named the PFA Player of the Year and the Football Writers' Association Footballer of the Year.

CRISTIANO RONALDO WAS JUST AS DEADLY IN EUROPE, WITH EIGHT GOALS IN 11 GAMES, AND IT WAS HIS POWERFUL HEADER THAT OPENED THE SCORING IN THE CHAMPIONS LEAGUE FINAL AGAINST CHELSEA.

# 2008 CHAMPIONS LEAGUE FINAL

The Champions League final in 2008, the only all-English final in the history of the competition, saw Manchester United and Chelsea make the long journey to Moscow to battle it out for the trophy.

The two league games between the sides that season had brought a 2-0 victory for United at Old Trafford and a 2-1 Chelsea triumph at Stamford Bridge, and the third and final clash between the pair in Russia was predictably tight.

The Red Devils drew first blood in the 26th minute when Cristiano Ronaldo rose highest in the box to power home a header from Wes Brown's cross, but The Blues struck back moments before half-time when Frank Lampard scored from close range.

THE CHAMPIONS LEAGUE FINAL IN 2008, THE ONLY ALL-ENGLISH FINAL IN THE HISTORY OF THE COMPETITION

The second 45 minutes and then 30 minutes of extra-time couldn't separate the two teams, and the final went to a penalty shoot-out.

Ronaldo missed with United's third spot-kick, but Chelsea skipper John Terry was off target with his team's fifth penalty when a goal would have won the contest for the London club. Ryan Giggs showed all his experience as he calmly converted United's seventh penalty, and when Edwin van der Sar saved Nicolas Anelka's subsequent effort, the Champions League trophy was on its way to Old Trafford for the third time in the club's history.

# 2008 CHAMPIONS LEAGUE CAMPAIGN

Manchester United's penalty shoot-out victory over Chelsea in the final of the 2008 Champions League was a personal triumph for Alex Ferguson, lifting the Scot into an exclusive group of managers to have won European club football's greatest prize twice.

His side's hard-fought victory over The Blues was also the fourth major piece of European silverware of Ferguson's Old Trafford reign, and brought to an end what the manager himself admitted had been a frustrating nine-year wait to add to the Champions League trophy his team had lifted back in 1999.

Ferguson shuffled his pack on a regular basis in the 13 games it took to be crowned European champions, using 23 players in total. No-one featured in all 13 fixtures, although midfielder Michael Carrick did start 11 times and come off the bench once during the course of the campaign.

The Red Devils scored 20 goals in Europe, with Cristiano Ronaldo's eight strikes earning him the Champions League Golden Boot award. Strikers Wayne Rooney and Carlos Tevez were the next highest-scoring United players with four goals each.

Ferguson's side were undefeated in all 13 of their European games, matching the feat they first achieved in 1998-99. Only Marseille, AC Milan, Ajax and Barcelona have done the same. The final was the eighth time the final had been settled by penalties and after making the match-winning stop at the death, United goalkeeper Edwin Van Der Sar was voted the UEFA Man of the Match.

# MANCHESTER UNITED:
# TOP TEN HEAVIEST DEFEATS

1. Manchester United 1-6 Manchester City, October 2011
2. Newcastle 5-0 Manchester United, October 1996
3. Southampton 6-3 Manchester United, October 1996
4. Chelsea 5-0 Manchester United, October 1999
5. Manchester United 0-3 Liverpool, March 2014
6. Middlesbrough 4-1 Manchester United, October 2005
7. Manchester United 1-4 Liverpool, March 2009
8. Manchester City 4-1 Manchester United, March 2004
9. Tottenham 4-1 Manchester United, January 1996
10. Leicester City 5-3 Manchester United, September 2014

# 08 FIFA CLUB WORLD CUP

Manchester United's win over Chelsea in the 2008 Champions League final earned them a place in the FIFA Club World Cup later in the year, and The Red Devils left for the Far East hoping to become the first English team to win the tournament since it began in 2000.

As the reigning European champions, United were given a bye in the quarter-finals but faced Gamba Osaka, the winners of the 2008 Asian Champions League, in the last four in the Yokohama International Stadium.

The match was an eight-goal thriller. Strikes from Nemanja Vidic and Cristiano Ronaldo in the first half gave United the edge, and although Gamaba pulled one back in the 74th minute, a three-goal blitz from Wayne Rooney, Darren Fletcher and a second from Rooney saw Alex Ferguson's side surge into a 5-1 lead late in the second half. There wasn't enough time for the Japanese side to recover, but they did score two goals in the final five minutes to entertain the crowd as United booked their place in the final with a 5-3 win.

The final against Ecuadorian club LDU Quito, winners of the 2008 Copa Libertadores, was in sharp contrast to the game before it. Only one goal separated the sides, and that goal went to United thanks to Rooney's smart 73rd-minute finish. Despite being reduced to ten men for much of the second half after Vidic was shown a red card, The Red Devils held out to earn the title of the world's best club side.

## THE FINAL AGAINST ECUADORIAN CLUB LDU QUITO, WINNERS OF THE 2008 COPA LIBERTADORES, WAS IN SHARP CONTRAST TO THE GAME BEFORE IT

# 2008-09 League

United's Premier League title win in 2008-09, their sixth of the decade, was a classic battle with old rivals Liverpool for the honours as Rafael Benitez's team tried to stop Alex Ferguson's side equalling the Merseysiders' record of 18 top-flight titles.

United made a poor start to the season, slipping to 15th in the table after their opening four league games. But The Red Devils slowly but surely found their feet, and by the New Year they were third. A 1-0 win at Bolton Wanderers in January, courtesy of a 90th-minute winner from Dimitar Berbatov, put United on top and Liverpool were unable to overhaul their arch-rivals.

WAYNE ROONEY WAS THE ONLY OTHER UNITED PLAYER TO REACH DOUBLE FIGURES IN THE LEAGUE, WITH 12 FOR THE SEASON

For the third season in a row, and in his last season with the club, Cristiano Ronaldo top-scored for the side with 18 Premier League goals. Wayne Rooney was the only other United player to reach double figures in the league, with 12 for the season.

The Red Devils also reached two cup finals, with contrasting results. In early March, the side beat Tottenham 4-1 on penalties in the final of the League Cup. But there was no fairytale ending in the Champions League final against Barcelona, as United's dreams of a fourth European crown were ended by a 2-0 defeat against the Catalan giants.

# 2010s

# THE 2010s

A decade which began with two more Premier League titles, the 2010s were also tinged with sadness as Manchester United said farewell to Alex Ferguson after 27 years of unprecedented success at Old Trafford under his leadership.

The manager finally parted company with the club after almost three decades of service in the summer of 2013, but before he moved upstairs to become a United director and club ambassador, Ferguson still had time to successfully secure three more trophies for The Red Devils.

The first came in 2010 in the shape of the League Cup, United overcoming Aston Villa 2-1 at Wembley thanks to goals from Michael Owen and Wayne Rooney. But having equalled Liverpool's record of 18 top-flight titles in 2009, it was another Premier League crown that Ferguson really wanted.

His side had finished runners-up to Chelsea in 2009-10, but the following year The Red Devils finally became the most successful team in the history of English league football when they won their 19th title, beating The Blues by nine points in a season which saw them lose just four times.

However, Ferguson wasn't happy with just setting a new record. The aim was to extend it, and in 2012-13, his last season as manager, his players gave

him the send-off he so richly deserved by being crowned champions once again. It was the 13th Premier League success of his career, a phenomenal record that many believe will never be beaten.

A new era in United's history began in May 2013, when it was announced Everton manager David Moyes would replace Ferguson. But he struggled to fill his fellow countryman's shoes and in April the following year, with the team sitting seventh in the table, the Scot was sacked.

Assistant manager Ryan Giggs took temporary charge until the end of the season, and in the summer of 2014 United confirmed the vastly-experienced Louis van Gaal, the former Barcelona, Bayern Munich and Holland manager, would take over.

The Dutchman signed a three-year deal with the club, and in his first season with The Red Devils he saw United qualify for the 2015-16 Champions League campaign after failing to do so the previous season.

A NEW ERA IN UNITED'S HISTORY BEGAN IN MAY 2013, WHEN IT WAS ANNOUNCED EVERTON MANAGER DAVID MOYES WOULD REPLACE FERGUSON

# PREMIER LEAGUE

|  | P | W | D | L | F | A | PTS | POS |
|---|---|---|---|---|---|---|---|---|
| 2009-10 | 38 | 27 | 4 | 7 | 86 | 28 | 85 | 2nd |
| 2010-11 | 38 | 23 | 11 | 4 | 78 | 37 | 80 | 1st |
| 2011-12 | 38 | 28 | 5 | 5 | 89 | 33 | 89 | 2nd |
| 2012-13 | 38 | 28 | 5 | 5 | 86 | 43 | 89 | 1st |
| 2013-14 | 38 | 19 | 7 | 12 | 64 | 43 | 64 | 7th |
| 2014-15 | 38 | 20 | 10 | 8 | 62 | 37 | 70 | 4th |

# HONOURS

**Premier League** 2010-11, 2012-13

**League Cup** 2010

**Community Shield** 2010, 2011, 2013

# BERBATOV

Signed from Tottenham Hotspur in the summer of 2008 in a £30.5million deal, Dimitar Berbatov enjoyed his best season in United colours in 2010-11, top-scoring for the club in the Premier League with 20 as The Red Devils were crowned champions.

The Bulgarian striker was on target in the opening fixture of the campaign, a 3-0 victory over Newcastle United at Old Trafford, and was on target in two of United's next three matches.

The two highlights of his season, however, were yet to come. The first was in September when his superb hat-trick sealed

a dramatic 3-2 victory over arch-rivals Liverpool. But in November, he was in even more devastating form when he hit a magnificent five past Blackburn in a 7-1 drubbing, a result which sent United top of the table for the first time that seaosn.

Not for the first time under Ferguson, United stayed in top spot for the remaining six months of the season. A 1-1 draw with Blackburn in May, thanks to a Wayne Rooney penalty, was enough to claim the title with a game to spare. Defending champions Chelsea were the runners-up, with Manchester City finishing third.

Berbatov's goals were crucial in the team's success, but it was also United's incredible form at Old Trafford that secured them the title. The Red Devils won 18 and drew one of their 19 league games at the Theatre of Dreams for a near 100 per cent home record.

# ROBIN VAN PERSIE

Striker Robin van Persie spent just three seasons at Old Trafford following his £24million arrival from Arsenal in 2012. But despite his short spell with the club, the Dutchman earned his place in United folklore in 2012-13 with a massive contribution as The Red Devils were crowned champions again.

The former Gunner featured in every league game under Alex Ferguson in his first season, and the Holland international repaid his manager's faith in style, top-scoring for United with 26 goals in 38 Premier League appearances.

Van Persie found the back of the net in just his second game for the club, a 3-2 win over Fulham at Old Trafford, and over the course of the season he hit hat-tricks against Southampton in September and Aston Villa in April. More importantly, he twice secured all three points with late winners against Liverpool at Anfield and Manchester City at the Etihad.

The Dutch forward, who played in the 2010 World Cup Final, completed the campaign with five goals in United's last seven league games, including a strike in Ferguson's final game in charge, a 5-5 draw with West Bromwich Albion at The Hawthorns. In all competitions, he scored 30 times.

Van Persie left in the summer of 2015, having scored 58 goals in 102 appearances for the club, an impressive strike rate of better than a goal every two games.

## "ROBIN VAN PERSIE BEST STRIKER IN THE WORLD."
MICHU

# 2012-13

Manchester United's 2012-13 Premier League crown was the 13th and final league triumph under Alex Ferguson. Fittingly, it was one of the most convincing title wins the Scot had masterminded, winning the crown back from neighbours Manchester City by 11 points.

A surprise 1-0 defeat to Everton at Goodison Park at the start of the season was only a temporary setback, and it sparked a superb sequence from The Red Devils. They won nine of their next 10 league games, which included a 2-1 victory over Liverpool at Anfield in September and 3-2 win over Chelsea at Stamford Bridge the following month.

In late November the team beat Queen Park Rangers 3-1 at Old Trafford with goals from Jonny Evans, Darren Fletcher and Javier Hernandez to take top spot, and despite the best efforts of Manchester City and Chelsea, the chasing pack were unable to catch Ferguson's team.

Robin van Persie led the way with 26 Premier League goals, while Wayne Rooney and Hernandez were the other United players to reach double figures with 12 and 10 respectively. The Red Devils were by far the division's deadliest attacking force with 86 goals in 38 games, 11 more than Chelsea and 20 more than City.

Van Persie made the most league starts for the club with 35, while Michael Carrick and Patrice Evra were just one behind on 34.

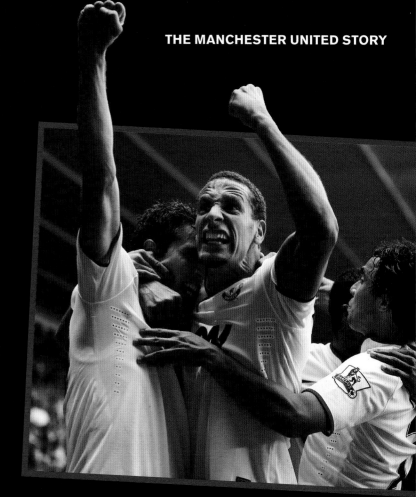

# 2012-13 PREMIER LEAGUE SEASON

It would have been a cruel end to such a glittering career if Alex Ferguson hadn't signed off with one last trophy triumph, and at the age of 71, the Scot was given the dream send-off as his side clinched the 2012-13 Premier League title.

THE MOUNTAIN OF SILVERWARE
FERGUSON WON AT OLD TRAFFORD
WILL PROBABLY NEVER BE BEATEN BY
ANOTHER MANAGER AT ANY OTHER CLUB

The 13th league victory of his career proved just as satisfying as his first two full decades earlier, and said everything about his desire to improve both the quality of squad and his own will to win.

His last ever match, a dramatic 5-5 draw with West Bromwich Albion in May, might not have gone to plan, but it mattered little as the Scot reflected on 27 remarkable years with The Red Devils.

The 13 league titles were incredible, but the tip of the iceberg. His five FA Cups and four League Cups underlined the domestic dominance United enjoyed under him, while two Champions League titles, victories in the UEFA Super Cup and the Cup Winners' Cup, as well the triumphs in the Intercontinental Cup and the FIFA Club World Cup, showed his sides could deliver in Europe too.

The mountain of silverware he won at Old Trafford will probably never be beaten by any other manager at any other club, and cements Ferguson's place as one of the greatest managers of all-time.

# DAVID MOYES

The Old Trafford faithful had high hopes for David Moyes when he took over from Alex Ferguson in 2013, but it was always going to be a daunting challenge and ultimately the former Everton boss was unable to fill the void left by Ferguson's retirement.

His first Premier League game saw The Red Devils beat Swansea 4-1 at the Liberty Stadium, and although his side shared the points with Chelsea at Old Trafford in the next match, tougher tests of the new manager lay ahead.

Defeats to Liverpool at Anfield and Manchester City at the Etihad put Moyes under early pressure. He railed the troops to register an eight-match unbeaten run in the league and a thumping 5-0 win in Germany against Bayer Leverkusen in the Champions League, but the improvement was short-lived.

HOME
TEAM

MANCHESTER UNITED

The month of April was to be his undoing. There was no disgrace in his side's 4-2 aggregate defeat to defending champions Bayern Munich in the quarter-finals of the Champions League, but when United then lost 2-0 in the league at his old club Everton, a result which meant The Red Devils couldn't qualify for the following season's Champions League, he was relieved of his duties.

MOYES HAD BEEN IN CHARGE FOR 51 GAMES, PICKING UP 27 WINS, BUT IT WASN'T ENOUGH AND ASSISTANT MANAGER RYAN GIGGS TOOK CHARGE FOR THE LAST FOUR FIXTURES OF THE CAMPAIGN

# LOUIS VAN GAAL

United's search for a new manager in 2014 was an extensive one, and in May the club announced they had secured the services of Louis van Gaal. The Dutchman arrived at Old Trafford later in the summer after guiding Holland to the semi-finals of the World Cup in Brazil, and the work began on rebuilding The Red Devils.

Aged 62 on his appointment and boasting over 20 years of experience, van Gaal began coaching in his native Holland with Ajax, winning three league titles and the 1992 UEFA Cup with the Dutch giants. In 1995 he claimed the Champions League trophy as well as the UEFA Super Cup and the Intercontinental Cup.

It was a sensational start to his managerial career. In 1997 he headed to Spain for the first of two stints at the Nou Camp with Barcelona, winning La Liga twice and another UEFA Super Cup with the Catalan club.

He was appointed Holland manager for a second time in 2012, steering the Dutch side through their ten World Cup qualifying games unbeaten. In the finals in Brazil, his side reached the last four and came within a whisker of reaching the final, only to lose in their semi-final against Argentina in a penalty shoot-out.

IT WAS A SENSATIONAL START TO HIS MANAGERIAL CAREER. IN 1997 HE HEADED TO SPAIN FOR THE FIRST OF TWO

# 2014-15
# WAYNE ROONEY

Having finished outside the Champions League places the previous season, Van Gaal's first task as Manchester United manager was to return the club back to Europe's top club competition.

The Dutchman did exactly that, as The Red Devils ended the season in fourth. It was an unspectacular campaign, but after the upheaval the previous year it was an encouraging start.

It owed much to Wayne Rooney. It was his 11th season in the famous red shirt, and for the 11th time of asking the England and United captain reached double figures in the Premier League with 12 goals, as well as top-scoring in all competitions with 14 goals from 37 appearances.

United had made a slow start under the new manager but Rooney was on hand when it mattered, scoring what proved to be the winner in a 2-1 triumph over Arsenal at the Emirates in late November. It was a result that took The Red Devils into the top four, and they stayed there for the rest of the season.

Rooney's goals continued to be vital. His opener against Liverpool in December kick-started a 3-0 win at Old Trafford, and he was on target twice later that month in a 3-1 triumph over Newcastle, while his goal against Aston Villa in April helped seal a 3-0 victory.

"HE GIVES US SOMETHING ELSE TO THINK ABOUT. HE'S A YOUNG PLAYER WITH REMARKABLE PHYSICAL AND CREATIVE POWER. HE HAS BELIEF AND DETERMINATION AND THE PHYSICAL ABILITY TO ACHIEVE WHAT HE SETS OUT TO DO."
## ARSENE WENGER, 2004

# 2015-16

# CHAMPIONS LEAGUE

Manchester United's fourth place finish in 2014-15 meant they had to negotiate a two-legged play-off to qualify for the 2015-16 Champions League group stages. The team were drawn against Belgian side Club Brugge, but secured a crushing 7-1 aggregate victory to reach the group stages.

United won the first leg at Old Trafford 3-1 thanks to two goals from Memphis Depay and a third from Marouane Fellaini, and they were even more dominant in the return leg as Wayne Rooney hit a brilliant hat-trick and Ander Herrera added a fourth to seal a 4-0 success. Their victory earned the team a place in Group B of the Champions League alongside PSV Eindhoven, Wolfsburg and CSKA Moscow.

It was the 20th season in which The Red Devils had qualified for the group stage of the competition, more than any other English club and a joint tournament record with Real Madrid, Barcelona and Porto. Although Van Gaal's team were beaten by PSV in their opening fixture, they underlined their European class with two wins and a draw in their next three games.

United are still the most successful Premier League side in the history of the Champions League, and will join an elite club of three-time winners the next time they lift the trophy.

**WAYNE ROONEY HIT A BRILLIANT HAT-TRICK AND ANDER HERRERA ADDED A FOURTH TO SEAL A 4-0 SUCCESS**

# CSKA MOSCOW

United's 1-0 win over CSKA Moscow in the group stages of the Champions League boosted the team's hopes of reaching the last 16, but Wayne Rooney's winner at Old Trafford had far greater significance for the United skipper.

Rooney's goal, a powerful second-half header from Jesse Lingard's cross, took his career tally for the club to 237. In the process, it took the striker level in joint second place on the all-time scoring list with the great Denis Law.

His strike came 11 years and two months after first scoring for The Red Devils. That day, his United debut against Fenerbahce in the Champions League at Old Trafford in September 2004, he went on to score a brilliant and memorable hat-trick.

ROONEY REACHED THE 237-GOAL MILESTONE AFTER 496 APPEARANCES FOR THE CLUB

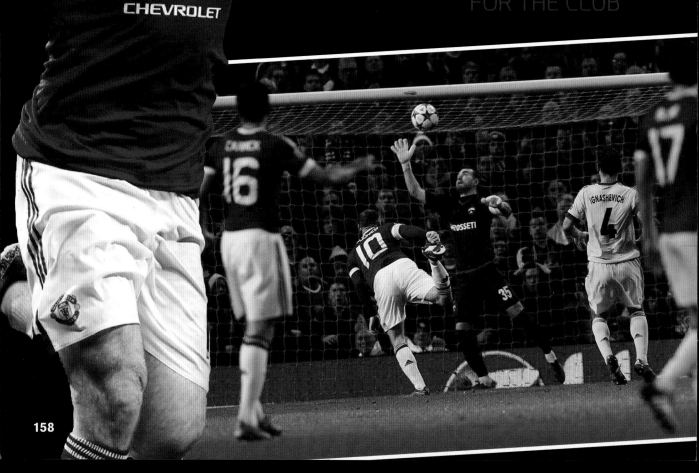

Rooney reached the 237-goal milestone after 496 appearances for the club, while Law got there in 404 games. When Rooney scored against CSKA Moscow he moved to within just 13 goals of Sir Bobby Charlton's long-standing record of 249 goals for the club.

The England star's two most lethal seasons for The Red Devils came in 2009-10 and 2011-12, when the he hit 34 goals in each campaign.

IN THE PROCESS, IT TOOK THE STRIKER LEVEL IN JOINT SECOND PLACE ON THE ALL-TIME SCORING LIST WITH THE GREAT DENIS LAW

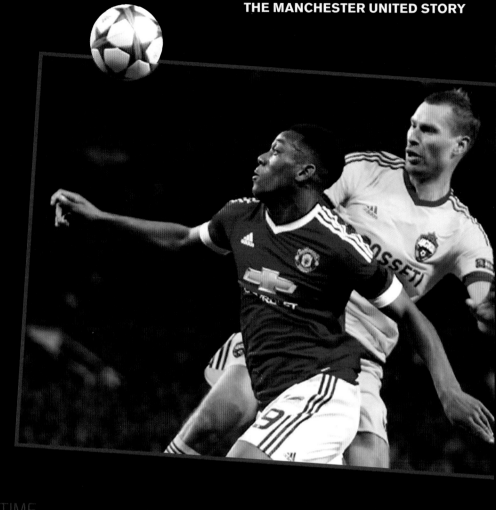

# MANCHESTER UNITED TROPHY CABINET

## PREMIER LEAGUE/ LEAGUE DIVISION ONE

| | |
|---|---|
| 1908-1909 | 1997-1998 |
| 1911-1912 | 1999-2000 |
| 1952-1953 | 2000-2001 |
| 1956-1957 | 2001-2002 |
| 1957-1958 | 2003-2004 |
| 1965-1966 | 2007-2008 |
| 1967-1968 | 2008-2009 |
| 1993-1994 | 2009-2010 |
| 1994-1995 | 2011-2012 |
| 1996-1997 | 2013-2014 |

## FA CUP

| | | |
|---|---|---|
| 1909-1910 | 1983-1984 | 1996-1997 |
| 1948-1949 | 1985-1986 | 1999-2000 |
| 1963-1964 | 1990-1991 | 2004-2005 |
| 1977-1978 | 1994-1995 | |

## FOOTBALL LEAGUE CUP

| | | | |
|---|---|---|---|
| 1992-1993 | 2006-2007 | 2009-2010 | 2010-2011 |

## FIFA CLUB WORLD CUP

| |
|---|
| 2008-2009 |

## FA CHARITY/ COMMUNITY SHIELD

| | | |
|---|---|---|
| 1908-1909 | 1977-1978* | 2003-2004 |
| 1911-1912 | 1983-1984 | 2007-2008 |
| 1952-1953 | 1990-1991* | 2008-2009 |
| 1956-1957 | 1993-1994 | 2010-2011 |
| 1957-1958 | 1994-1995 | 2011-2012 |
| 1965-1966* | 1996-1997 | 2013-2014 |
| 1967-1968* | 1997-1998 | *-shared |

## EUROPEAN CUP/ UEFA CHAMPIONS LEAGUE

| | | |
|---|---|---|
| 1968-1969 | 1999-2000 | 2008-2009 |

## EUROPEAN CUP WINNERS' CUP

| |
|---|
| 1991-1992 |

## UEFA SUPER CUP

| |
|---|
| 1991-1992 |